www.silencedturkey.org

FREEDOM CONVENTION

GRAVE HUMAN RIGHTS VIOLATIONS IN TURKEY

HAFZA GIRDAP

MARCH 2022

ADVOCATES OF SILENCED TURKEY

AST is a 501(c)(3) tax exempt, not for profit charitable and educational organization based in New Jersey, USA exclusively for defending human and civil rights.

EIN: 83-1568246

MAILING ADDRESS

Advocates of Silenced Turkey
P.O. Box 2399
Wayne, NJ 07474-2399

CONTACT

✉ help@silencedturkey.org

WEB & SOCIAL MEDIA

www.silencedturkey.org
@silencedturkey
facebook.com/silencedturkey
youtube.com/advocatesofsilencedturkey

EDITOR
HAFZA GIRDAP

ASSISTANT EDITORS
TAYLOR QUALLS
NEDA YILDIRIM

ILLUSTRATOR
MUHSIN NAZIF

VISUAL MEDIA DIRECTOR
SERKAN TAYFUR

ORGANIZATION COMMITTEE
HAFZA GIRDAP, NEDA YILDIRIM,
SABAHATTIN TOPRAK, MUSTAFA BAHAR,
ESRA NUR, MEHMET KAVAL

COPYRIGHT © AST PUBLISHING, 2022

All publication rights of this work belong to the Advocates of Silenced Turkey Inc. and AST Publishing. All rights reserved. No part of this book may be reproduced or transmitted in any form or by any means, electronic or mechanical, including photocopying, recording or by any information storage and retrieval system without permission in writing from the Advocates of Silenced Turkey Inc.

TABLE OF CONTENTS

GRAVE HUMAN RIGHTS VIOLATIONS IN TURKEY — 9

FREEDOM OF EXPRESSION AND SPEECH — 10
- ÖMER FARUK GERGERLİOĞLU — 12
- EUGENE CHUDNOVSKY — 15
- ARZU YILDIZ — 18
- ABDÜLHAMİT BİLİCİ — 21

COLLAPSE OF RULE OF LAW — 24
- DAVID KILGOUR — 25
- Y. ALP ASLANDOĞAN — 30
- KISTEN KRISH GOVENDER — 34
- JAMES HARRINGTON — 37

SHIFT FROM DEMOCRATIZATION TOWARDS AUTHORITARIANISM IN TURKEY: THE RISE OF POLITICAL ISLAM — 41
- ALON BEN MEIR — 42
- BÜLENT KENEŞ — 46
- RABIA CHAUDRY — 51

POWER, POLITICAL VIOLENCE, AND VIOLATIONS OF MINORITY RIGHTS IN TURKEY — 54
- SÜMEYYE AVCI — 55
- MICHAEL RUBIN — 57
- CRAIG R. SHAGIN — 60
- BÜLENT CEYHAN — 63
- KERİM BALCI — 66

TABLE OF CONTENTS

MEHMET EFE ÇAMAN	70
WOMEN'S RIGHTS IN TURKEY	**73**
EREN KESKIN, Esq.	74
HİLAL AKDENİZ	77
VONYA WOMACK	81
ARLET NATALI AVAZYAN	84
SOPHIA PANDYA	87
PROMOTING CIVIL AND POLITICAL RIGHTS	**90**
RUTH BEN-GHIAT	91
ARBANA XHARRA	94
MFANA GWALA	96
THE CRACKDOWN ON RULE OF LAW	**99**
ARAT BARIŞ	100
SERDAR ÇELEBİ	104
YASEMİN MAMALOĞLU	108
DISCRIMINATORY GOVERNMENT POLICIES AGAINST MINORITIES, ETHNICITIES, DISSIDENTS	**112**
DAVID PHILLIPS	113
MELTEM ARIKAN	117
BÜŞRA NİSA SARAÇ	121
ANJEL DİKME	123
DESPINA SYRRI	126

FREEDOM CONVENTION

WHO WE ARE

AST is a 501(c)(3) Not for Profit charitable and educational organization based in NJ, exclusively for defending human and civil rights.

Our aim is,

- To address all forms of human rights violations being perpetrated in Turkey including civil, political, economic, social and cultural-- based on the tenets upheld in fundamental human rights documents;

- To speak up against any forms of genocide, crimes against humanity, arbitrary detentions, cases of torture and ill treatment, and discrimination, and stand up for principles and values such as the right to life, the rule of law, the right to privacy, freedom of expression, freedom of thought, conscience and religion, and freedom of associations;

- To utilize all human rights advocacy tools, mechanisms, and systems that can possibly be utilized in order to protect and demand the fundamental human rights of those whose voices are being silenced in Turkey and beyond;

- And to hold accountable the perpetrators who are denying individuals in Turkey and beyond their fundamental Human Rights while providing the victims with the opportunity to obtain justice and reparation.

In order to do so, we use the power of the law to fight the impunity of the perpetrators, their accomplices and the instigators of these crimes; we defend the interests of the victims before both national and international courts and we bring specific cases before the appropriate international human rights bodies, working in close collaboration with local partners and the victims themselves to make sure that the authorities take firm action against such violations.

FREEDOM CONVENTION

GRAVE HUMAN RIGHTS VIOLATIONS IN TURKEY

Turkey Freedom Forum is a unique convention for human rights activists, intellectuals, and policymakers focused on human rights violations in Turkey organized by AST. In pursuance of justice and peace, this forum aims to bring hundreds of human rights defenders and activists together and to foster the dynamics to mobilize. This report will focus on five unique panel topics and will highlight outstanding discussions. ■

FREEDOM CONVENTION

FREEDOM OF EXPRESSION AND SPEECH

The dictionary meaning of **"freedom"** is the power or right to act, speak, or think as one wants without hindrance or restraint. Over the last four years, Turkey has been immersed in a deepening human rights crisis, with a catastrophic loss of its rule of law and democratic foundation. In Turkey, executive authority and political influence over the judiciary has resulted in courts accepting fabricated indictments, detaining and convicting individuals who are viewed as political opponents without any strong proof of criminal behavior or any regard for procedural fairness in law, access to justice, restricted use of pretrial detention. There is an emerging widespread consensus among scholars and journalists over the nature of the political regime in Turkey. One chief assumption rests at the center of countless diverse studies - Turkey is no longer a democracy and there is little space for the right to act, speak or think.

The Freedom Convention Turkey 2020 and 2021, as the signature event of Advocates of Silenced Turkey (AST), brought 45 prominent panelists from different disciplines together to shed light on the ongoing overall democratic backsliding in the Republic of Turkey. The Convention scrutinized the deterioration of free expression in Turkish civil society, liberty and security abductions, and forced disappearances. Speakers also focused on renditions of dissenters, discriminatory government policies against minorities rights as a result of Turkish government's increasingly more violent use of political and military power against dissidents, members of the opposition, and regular civilians. The convention illuminated the deterioration of the rule of law in the Republic of Turkey and its effects on the judiciary system along with guidance on the importance of building a vocal democracy by establishing better safeguards for universal human rights, more robust institutions for the protection of independent law, social acceptance of different ideologies and peaceful dissent. ■

FREEDOM CONVENTION

FREEDOM CONVENTION

ÖMER FARUK GERGERLİOĞLU

Ömer Faruk Gergerlioglu is a medical doctor, human rights activist, and MP of the People's Democratic Party (HDP). He has dedicated his political career to fighting against human rights violations in Turkey.

Humanity's ultimate potential is revealed when we are given space for full freedom of expression. Since we first walked the planet we have been communicating with one another, attempting to externalize our internal world. Perhaps it was in those early days when our expression was truly at its freest. Summoning our collective hopes, dreams, and goals, as well as the stuff of daily life, we left a lasting mark on the walls of caves. As society grew ever more complex, some found their voices silenced, their hopes and sufferings lost to the world outside. Throughout history, it has been those who see injustice and speak against it that are first to be silenced. Oppression often begins as a muzzle, but muzzling inevitably gives way to far more insidious consequences for speaking against injustice: the loss of property, the stripping away of basic rights, and ultimately the theft of human life.

With unchecked power at their disposal, time and time again powerful oppressors throughout the world have lashed out at those who cry out for freedom and in doing so have struck blows not just against individuals but against human progress. Whether operating in the political, religious, scientific, or social realms, it is these very lovers of freedom who pave the way for our advancement. They create new proposals and projects, new ways of thinking about our world, and wherever their voices are silenced, we all suffer as a result.

We do not have time to recount thousands of years of human history, nor do I believe you need a history lesson. We all recognize that tyrants have silenced the voices of freedom lovers for a reason: it is through the power of expression and those who are not afraid to lift their voices that oppression, injustice, and tyranny are put to an end. While words alone do not topple dictators, we can all see that every time humanity has embraced freedom, the struggle began with words not weapons, and in the end, it is upon the ideals of freedom and those who uphold its values that thriving societies are built.

It is easy to see this narrative through the line of freedom and oppression throughout all of human history, but today I want to focus on its relevance for Turkey, where those who value freedom and human progress all must presently turn their attention. Turkey is a country that encountered democracy much later. The Republic of Turkey arose out of the collapse of the Ottoman Empire, whose people were riddled with trauma and pain. A Republic in name, the newly founded country found freedom of expression dangerous as it attempted to salvage what was left of the legacy of the empire. Those in power chiseled a place for themselves into the foundation of the new country and the voiceless masses suffered greatly. In this new "Republic" Muslims could not say "Allah", Christians were silenced, Alevis were fearful for their lives if they were identified in any way with their sect, and Kurds were condemned simply for speaking in their mother tongue. Only those in power could have their say and anyone who spoke otherwise suffered the most severe of consequences.

Even as those in power attempted to control both the thought and language of the people, there were still examples of free-thinking, civilized discussion, and the expression of diverging opinions to be found in the margins. There were groups whose ideologies traditionally opposed one another who found a common goal in the desire for freedom. Whether captured on TV in a moment of dissent or shouting the message of freedom on a street corner, those who spoke out against tyranny fearlessly paid the ultimate price, but they have not been forgotten. These poets, writers, politicians, and ordinary people are remembered even now as they inspire us to continue in our fight for freedom in Turkey.

Unfortunately, in the intervening years, the situation has not improved. In 2016 Turkish leaders declared a state of emergency, seizing total control of the government and undermining the constitution, for that state of emergency persists to this day. People from all different walks of life, as well as political and religious commitments, are speaking in agreement that freedom has never been so completely threatened in Turkey as it is right now. Touting its high value of human life and freedom, Turkey has backtracked any gains that it actually made in recent decades. Free thought and open debate in Turkey have all but disappeared as evidenced by the droves of young people who delete social media profiles out of fear of displeasing President Erdoğan and being labeled an enemy of the state because "big brother" is watching everywhere. Even one's ability to gain employment in the public sector is deeply impacted by the way that individuals speak of the president.

Over the last four years, we have become a country of people whose houses are raided by police in the early hours of the morning, whose children are tortured before our fearful eyes. The figures speak for themselves, in four and a half years there have been over 600,000 investigations, 300,000 detentions, and 100,000 arrests. Special laws enacted by our government allow them to restrict and police social media as they see fit, are a country of people who are humiliated and mistreated for criticism of the government that occurred years ago. >>>

FREEDOM CONVENTION

FREEDOM CONVENTION

This has given us a generation of hopeless children, and how could this not be the case when any act can be declared an act of terrorism simply because the government declares it so. At this point, we are the country with the most incarcerated babies in the world.

The specific stories of individuals who have had their rights violated by the Turkish government could fill a library, but it seems most fitting that here I turn to my own story. At one point the Prosecutor's Office put a case before Parliament claiming that I was making propaganda for a terrorist organization because I had been present during a speech given by the HDP leader Selhattin Demirtas. Another report about me, prepared by the Ankara Chief Public Prosecutor's Office, was filed because I made a public report that a prisoner with COVİD-19 was hospitalized. Even after the prisoner died due to COVİD-19, the government remained silent as to their fate and did not retract the accusations against me. Many other journalists have lived through similar experiences over the past few years as the government has disseminated lies and attempted to cover up the reality of the pandemic. As a parliamentarian with immunity, I was subjected to actual police beatings during many of my press releases, and again I am not the only politician to have my rights violated so flagrantly.

Finally, I turn to the somewhat ironic fact that the book Freedom of Expression, which was penned by esteemed human rights defenders and lawyers like the head of the country's Constitutional Court, Zühtü Arslan, and which was legally published and sold, is banned from Diyarbakır prison during the State of Emergency. It was banned because those in charge of the prison declared it terrorist propaganda. I live in a country that has confused free expression for terrorism and perceives truth as a threat. It will only be through the unchaining of such free expression that Turkey can thrive and contribute to the global community.

> "I live in a country that has confused free expression for terrorism and perceives truth as a threat. It will only be through the unchaining of such free expression that Turkey can thrive and contribute to the global community."

EUGENE CHUDNOVSKY

Eugene Michael Chudnovsky is a Distinguished Professor of Physics at Herbert H. Lehman College of the City University of New York and a Fellow of the American Physical Society (APS). The denial by the USSR of an exit visa to Chudnovsky in 1979 led to his unemployment for eight years. He was frequently harassed and interrogated by the KGB. He has been an active defender of human rights.

By the numbers Turkey has been accused of the most human rights violations of any modern country. What follows is merely a sampling of the Turkish government's crimes.

In the fall of 2015, Turkey used tanks and helicopters to suppress a Kurdish insurgency in the country's southeast. An observer, known to the CCS, visited the area and wrote: "The scale of the losses and the destruction suffered by the civilian population could only be comprehended as a collective punitive operation against the inhabitants, a measure that has no place in any modern legal system." She cited a local newspaper describing the death of a 14-year-old boy who had gone out to fetch water from a nearby quarter: "Based on eyewitness accounts, he was shot in the chest and fell. He raised his hand to signal he was still alive. They shot him in the hand. Then one officer walked up to him and shot him in the head."

In January 2016, over 2,000 scholars (1,128 Turkish academics among them) signed the petition "We Will Not Be a Part of this Crime", drafted by Turkish Academics for Peace, a group advocating for a peaceful solution to the Kurdish issue since 2012. Over 600 of the signers have since been put on trial and more than 140 of them have been sentenced to prison terms ranging from 15 to 36 months. Dr. Şebnem Korur Fincancı of the Institute of Forensic Medicine, President of the Turkish Human Rights Foundation, known for her work for the UN War Crime Tribunal in Bosnia, was sentenced to 30 months in December 2018. Physicist Ayşe Erzan, recipient of the 2003 L'Oreal-UNESCO Award for Women in Science and of the 2009 European Rammal Award, was sentenced to 15 months. >>>

FREEDOM CONVENTION

FREEDOM CONVENTION

On July 26, 2019, the Turkish Constitutional Court ruled that sentences given to Academics for Peace who protested the massacre of Kurdish civilians by the Turkish army violated their freedom of expression. The court also ruled that each of the accused be paid 9,000 Turkish lira (about $1,600) in damages incurred during the investigation, trials, and imprisonment. In October 2019, Ayşe Erzan was awarded the Andrei Sakharov prize of the American Physical Society.

NASA scientist and U.S. citizen Serkan Gölge was arrested on a family visit in the Hatay province of Turkey in the summer of 2016. The first court hearing took place on April 17, 2017, nearly a year later. Gölge was accused of membership in the organization of Fethullah Gülen and spying for the CIA. Material evidence of his "crimes" included his teenage studies at the Test Preparation Center and Fatih University in Istanbul (now closed by Erdoğan) allegedly affiliated with Gülen, as well as his account in Bank Asya (also closed), that was popular with Gülen's supporters. The serial number of a one-dollar bill found in Gölge's possession at the time of his arrest was interpreted as his place in the hierarchy of Gülen's organization. Gölge denied all charges. Two other hearings in May and July 2017 ended similarly. He was sentenced to 7.5 years in prison (decreased to 5 years in Sept 2018) for allegedly providing material support to Gülen's organization.

While in prison, Gölge developed kidney stones and was hospitalized for three days. A request by his attorney to release him on bail was denied by the judge. According to the attorney, the interrogators repeatedly asked Gölge whether he would be willing to return to the U.S. as a spy for Turkey in exchange for freedom.

Gölge came to the U.S. in 2003. He attended a graduate program at Old Dominion University in Norfolk, Va., and did his doctoral and postdoctoral studies at the Thomas Jefferson National Accelerator Facility. He became an American citizen in 2010. In 2013, he worked as a senior scientist at the University

> **According to the attorney, the interrogators repeatedly asked Gölge whether he would be willing to return to the U.S. as a spy for Turkey in exchange for freedom.**

of Houston and did research for NASA's Johnson Space Center. He married his sweetheart, Kübra, who came to the U.S. from Turkey to study English literature. They bought a house in Houston where they lived with their two sons before his arrest in Turkey. Gölge was released in May 2019 following a phone conversation between U.S President Trump and Erdoğan. For more than a year he was kept under house arrest. He was finally allowed to return to the U.S. in July 2020.

Tuna Altınel is a mathematics professor at France's Claude Bernard Lyon 1 University. In February 2019 he attended a meeting of the "Amitiés Kurdes de Lyon", a French organization that raises awareness about the plight of the Kurds. At this meeting, the film Cizîr Djizre Cizre was projected, and a Turkish politician Faysal Sarıyıldız, who is a member of the Turkish People's Democratic Party (HDP), delivered a speech.

In April 2019, Professor Altınel traveled to Turkey to spend his holiday. On his entry to the country, his passport was confiscated. On May 10, 2019, when he came to a police precinct to inquire about his passport, he was arrested and accused of "propagandizing for a terrorist organization".

Professor Altınel had lived and worked in France since 1996. His arrest ignited numerous protests from mathematicians and human rights organizations around the world. In July 2019 he was released from prison and was acquitted of all charges in January 2020. However, his request to the authorities in Balıkesir to re-issue his passport was denied in a letter dated September 2020, making it impossible for him to return to his teaching duties in France.

FREEDOM CONVENTION

FREEDOM CONVENTION

ARZU YILDIZ

An outspoken journalist, Arzu Yıldız had to leave Turkey due to a number of cases filed against her for her news reports that drew the ire of the Turkish government. Yıldız currently lives in Canada.

I was born in Turkey and grew up there. I spent 36 formative years calling Turkey home and have seen many countries of the world but I never planned to leave, until 4 years ago.

I was a journalist working in an alternative media organization. Dedicated to writing, I set aside financial gains and spent a lot out of my own pocket. I worked as a court reporter, so I didn't read the horrors in the newspapers; I experienced them as I heard victims. I didn't just hear their stories, I felt them. In the Ankara Station attack, I saw the shattered human bodies and the families waiting to receive mutilated corpses of lost loved ones.

I wrote for the Taraf newspaper until 2013 and witnessed so many shocking stories play out. Among these, numerous revolved around corruption files such as Deniz Feneri, which the government followed closely. Others followed unsolved murder cases against Kurdish businessmen. On December 17th the corruption investigation came to light. Among those named in this case were ministers and members of Erdoğan's family. In the days following, on January 1st and 19th, I witnessed the arrest of the four prosecutors who uncovered the crime of arms smuggling in Adana. But unlike others, I refused to stay quiet. I attempted to publicize this display of unlawful injustice and share the story with anyone who would listen. Many people chose to ignore these events, thinking to 'let sleeping dogs lie' would do no harm. Sadly, this silence helped no one and they were quiet until July 15th, 2016 [the failed coup attempt]. They kept silent, anxious to keep their salaries and positions. The fire of injustice, which was sparked that July, became real flames and burned the houses of many educated people. When the fire finally engulfed their homes, they started screaming and what they feared most came to fruition. From that fateful day, like these homes, the law in Turkey has gone up in flames, scorching everything in its path.

The deep state spent many years hiding behind the government, biding their time, before greed took over and their plans broke out. This brutal mob, which tagged its own people according to their ideology, race, lifestyle, and gender declared them enemies. Thousands of people were wrongly imprisoned, more than 3,000 judges and prosecutors among them, in one night. This dismal figure reached 6,000. All of a sudden, books were considered evidence of a crime. Anyone who refused to accept the terms of the deep state in Turkey was arrested and imprisoned. Even today, reading the book of HDP's imprisoned leader Demirtaş is considered a terrorist crime in Turkey. This is what the rulers of the state say.

The vicious fire blazed and the people of Turkey were engulfed. The flame only grows with each passing day, demanding more and more to feed it. Because the shallow mindset – that is, the mindset that looks at your ethnicity or religion before your humanity – doesn't take your victimhood seriously. People are intimidated by the news of torture and lament over lost careers, money, and comfort, which they believe makes a life worth living. This mindset impacts the mood of other people.

I openly criticize the system before individuals and institutions without apology. I have no problem with Erdoğan and AKP. They are a cog in the corrupted system. There are international press organizations in Turkey. They are of no real help. PEN (poets, essayists, and novelists) and similar organizations may not be putting money in their own pockets, these institutions commit the crime of discrimination. They portray whoever they want as victims. They are of no use. I haven't received a single message from any of them in four years. I don't believe they're sincerely worried about the plight of others nor do they understand the devastating situations at hand. They haven't been able to effect any change.

Upon leaving Turkey, I went to Canada. At the time, my children were 7 months and 7 years old. Lots of people live together here in >>>

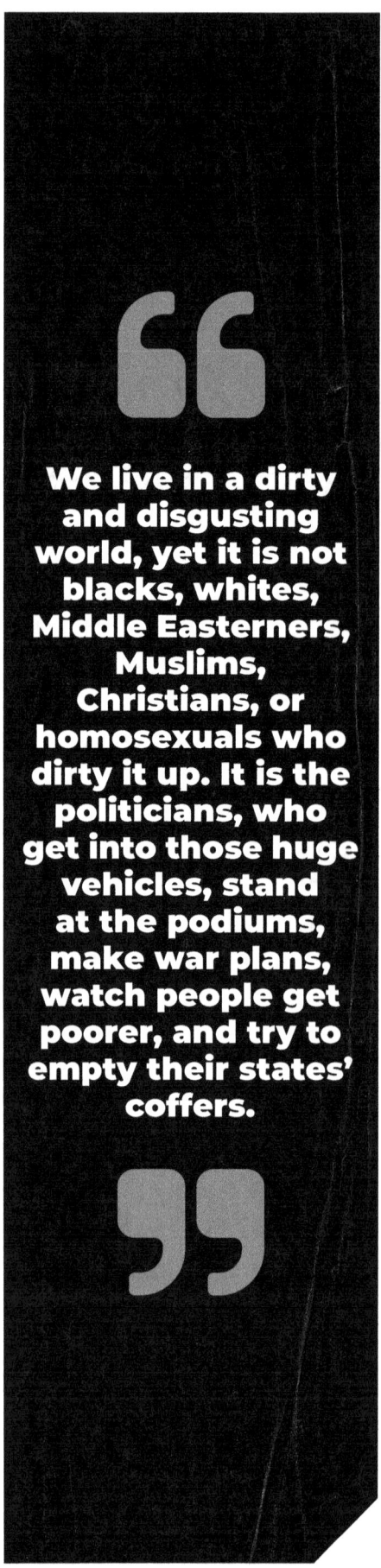

> We live in a dirty and disgusting world, yet it is not blacks, whites, Middle Easterners, Muslims, Christians, or homosexuals who dirty it up. It is the politicians, who get into those huge vehicles, stand at the podiums, make war plans, watch people get poorer, and try to empty their states' coffers.

FREEDOM CONVENTION

FREEDOM CONVENTION

Canada without the daily fear we lived within Turkey. Law and justice are assured here, and there is no problem.

I believe that democracy in the world is a big lie and hypocrisy. I see no honor and dignity in judges or prosecutors. The President of the ECtHR goes to Turkey and poses for pictures. In the country where he stood for a photograph, members of the court have been held in solitary confinement for four years. There are nearly 100 detained judges and prosecutors only 16 kilometers away, Hiigh judges are held in solitary cells 130 kilometers away. Who can tell me this man is a man of law? Who can claim that this man has any respect for his profession? How can a person, who does not defend his profession and honor humans, live claim to be just?

We live in a dirty and disgusting world, yet it is not blacks, whites, Middle Easterners, Muslims, Christians, or homosexuals who dirty it up. It is the politicians, who get into those huge vehicles, stand at the podiums, make war plans, watch people get poorer, and try to empty their states' coffers. None of them is my leader.

I don't need any leader. The world needs people to live humanely. Colorful like a rainbow, not black and white. Leaders who claim that death is sacred are not the ones dying. They establish borders and force us to leap over the fences. They kill us on the road.

Turkey is where I was born and lived for a while. Canada is, however, where I currently live. I don't know what happens next, and I refuse to have a nation, religion, or label define me. I am a human being who is appealing for justice in Turkey. Demanding justice for the broken bodies and minds still fighting for a human existence free of punishment for reading a book. I just want to live and die as a human being. The people of Turkey deserve that too.

ABDÜLHAMİT BİLİCİ

Abdülhamit Bilici served as editor-in-chief of the Zaman daily, which was Turkey's highest-selling newspaper until it was seized by the Turkish government with a police raid. He also held top managerial positions in Cihan News Agency and Aksiyon Weekly Magazine. He currently lives in the U.S. after having to escape from the Erdoğan regime's persecution.

These are very bad times for Turkey in terms of democracy. I am an exiled journalist, living in the U.S. for the last 4 years - since 2016. I was the last Editor in Chief of Zaman daily, which was the highest circulated newspaper in Turkey. To clarify and help the international community understand the gravity of the confiscation of my newspaper, I offer this example. Imagine the French government confiscating Le Monde or the U.S. government shutting down the Washington Post and their chief editors being forced to flee the country.

Of course, the persecution and silencing of journalists is not limited to my newspaper. There are today more than 100 journalists behind bars and in the last 3 years, more than 200 media outlets were shut down, outlets representing different perspectives of Turkish society. Some of them were liberal, some were Kurdish or leftists, etc., but the common thing about them was that they were critical of the government. My story is not important because it is mine, but because it represents an important picture of what's going on in Turkey.

We were preparing to celebrate our 13th year as a newspaper and we were supporting Turkey in its process of becoming a real democracy and joining the European Union. It was one of my editorial priorities to bring different voices to speak their minds without any limitations. On a normal day, you could see in our newspaper a journalist or columnist from Kurdish background, from a leftist background, from a liberal background expressing their opinions on the same topic. There was a richness to Turkey's intellectual life. Since 2013, when the great corruption scandal was revealed, our newspaper started to be very critical of the government. >>>

FREEDOM CONVENTION

FREEDOM CONVENTION

This created a rift and tension between the government and our platform. Most of our columnists, reporters, and staff struggled from 2013 until March of 2016. Despite all the pressure, for instance, the court cases, the threats, the cancellation of press cards, or inspections by financial auditors, I'm proud that all our staff and journalists stood strong until March 4th, 2016. It was then that a court appointed trustees to our newspaper.

They did not come in a civilized way; it was an occupation by a brutal police force against journalists, who had done nothing other than writing their opinions. They converted the newspaper from a critical voice to a mouthpiece of the government and of course, they fired me immediately. Our daily release was now a kind of propaganda brochure that lasted for 4 months until the coup attempt on July 15. They ridiculously accused our newspaper, which was under control at that time, of supporting the coup and they raided the houses of our columnists and reporters and arrested whoever they found.

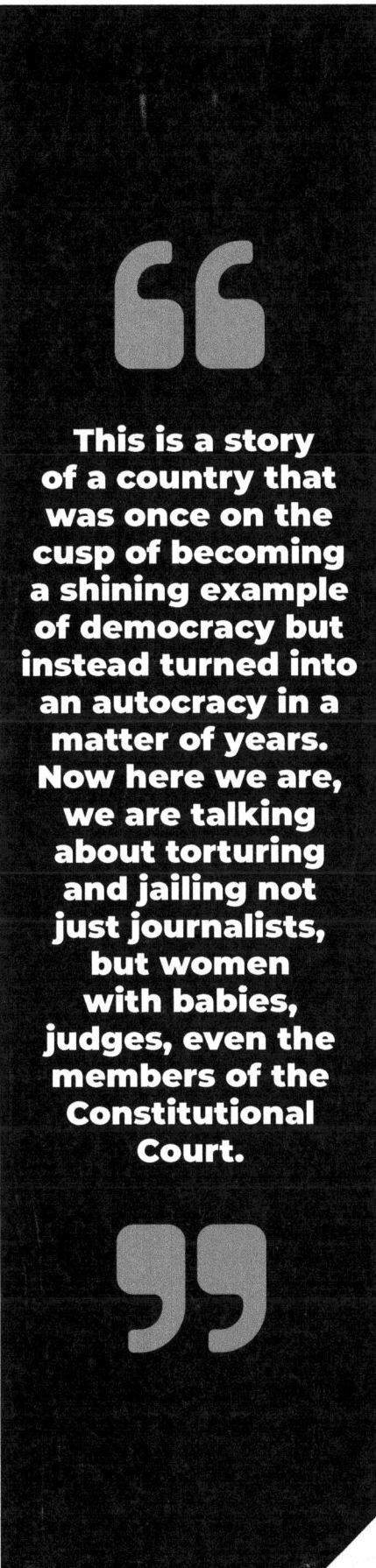

> **This is a story of a country that was once on the cusp of becoming a shining example of democracy but instead turned into an autocracy in a matter of years. Now here we are, we are talking about torturing and jailing not just journalists, but women with babies, judges, even the members of the Constitutional Court.**

As I share my story I am ashamed to look back and remember those who faced prison terms or torture. This is a story of a country that was once on the cusp of becoming a shining example of democracy but instead turned into an autocracy in a matter of years. Now here we are, we are talking about torturing and jailing not just journalists, but women with babies, judges, even the members of the Constitutional Court. The question is, how did that happen. In my view, a very important reason is an incorrect diagnosis of the problem. If you hope to solve a problem, you need to have a good and correct diagnosis of the problem first. When this oppression and the drift of the Turkish government away from democracy began in 2013 with the Gezi protests in the summer of 2013 and then with the corruption scandal in December of the same year, many people in Turkey, including international observers, defined the problem as a power struggle between the Gülen movement and the government. This incorrect diagnosis of the problem alienated a lot

of people in Turkey who were supposed to come together against the drift from democracy, against authoritarian policies.

Since it was an incorrect definition, it did not stop there. An overwhelming majority of the persecution and violations are against members of the Gülen movement today with more than 1.3 million people being investigated and more than 300,000 of them arrested. But, this problem is not limited to them. When you look at the people in jails today, you can see many others from different walks of life, persecuted for their opposition to the government, like philanthropist and businessman Osman Kavala or the HDP leader Selahattin Demirtaş.

When you look at Turkey, you see that this pattern of human rights violations and the destruction of democracy is not new. We had a one-party rule for 25 years at the beginning of the Republic and in those years, like today, conservative religious people were in jail together with leftists, liberals, etc. We should also remember the persecution against the Armenians, the Jews, the Kurds, etc. So, what we are witnessing in Turkey today is not new, it is repeating itself over and over again, and this brings me to the point that I want to underline: why are we not learning from our mistakes? We are living the darkest times because, for instance, in the past, the autocrats didn't touch the wives and kids. Now, however, the Turkish jails have more than 10,000 women and more than 700 babies. Yes, Turkey has never been a democratic country but today, it is much darker than in past eras. ■

FREEDOM CONVENTION

FREEDOM CONVENTION

COLLAPSE OF
RULE OF LAW

DAVID KILGOUR

> David Kilgour is the former Secretary of State for Latin America and Africa (1997-2002) and Asia-Pacific (2002-2003) in the cabinet of Prime Minister Jean Chretien. He represented southeast Edmonton in the House of Commons from 1979 to 2006 during eight Parliaments. He has a passion for multi-party democracy, human rights, and justice for all. He stepped down as a Member of Parliament in 2006 to become an advocate for human dignity and good governance internationally. He and David Matas were nominated in 2010 for the Nobel Peace Prize for their book, Bloody Harvest, and campaign to end party-state-run organ abuse across China.

Turkey has long been admired internationally as a Muslim-majority democracy with an industrious people and a strong economy. Under World War I hero and founder, Mustafa Kemal Atatürk, Turks obtained full independence in 1923, and later the rule of law, universal literacy, separation of state and religion, equal rights for women, and a strategically important NATO membership.

Governing in the Atatürk tradition in their early years, Recep Tayyip Erdoğan and his Justice and Development Party (AKP) impressed many at home and abroad. He was elected mayor of Istanbul (1994), prime minister (2003- 2014), and president (2014). The economic well-being of many Turks improved markedly in his first five years as prime minister. Other achievements included temporarily winding down a 30-year conflict with Turkey's 15-million-strong Kurdish minority and accepting large numbers of refugees from Bashar al-Assad's Syria.

In 2013, however, when a corruption scandal broke out involving Erdoğan and his cabinet, no one was charged. Judges, prosecutors, and police were quickly re-assigned. Fethullah Gülen, cleric and founder of the Gülen Movement (GM), also known as Hizmet, who had supported him when they both sought membership in the European Union and further democratization of Turkey, broke with him that year and the GM was subsequently was declared "a terrorist" by Erdoğan. >>>

FREEDOM CONVENTION

FREEDOM CONVENTION

American academic Sophia Pandya describes the GM as:

"a Sufism-inspired, civil society, humanitarian organization ... [with] thousands of educational, charitable, and cultural organizations [globally] ... Gülen has ... denied any personal or institutional involvement [in the attempted coup]. If there are ... officers among the coup plotters who consider themselves... sympathizer[s] of [GM], [they] committed treason against the unity of [Turkey] by [participating] in an event where their own citizens lost their lives."

The full details of the attempted coup on July 15, 2016, might never be fully known. A group of mid-ranking Turkish soldiers seized control of the Parliament in Ankara along with Istanbul's bridges, airports, and some police stations. Citizens, including police, courageously overpowered them although 250 persons perished during the ensuing violence.

Unfortunately for Turkey and the world, Erdoğan used the attempted coup to subvert democracy, which Turks have fought for over 93 years, to achieve increasingly totalitarian goals. Like Putin in Russia, Erdoğan has since sought to create some formal, but shallow, institutions of democracy. Research by Burak Bekdil (Nov 2020) indicates that 38% of Turks consider they no longer belong in Turkey. The Economist (Nov. 21-27) indicates that Berat Albayrak, Erdoğan's son-in-law, nearly ruined the economy of Turkey before quitting.

The Stockholm Center for Freedom (www.stockholmcf.org) observed after the coup:

"freedoms in Turkey have been suspended, 150,000 civil servants accused of having dissident views have been purged on terror charges, censorship of the media has reached alarming levels, and [more than] ... 50,000 soldiers, prosecutors, police officers, diplomats, academics, journalists, business people, lawyers, doctors, teachers, students, and housewives have been arrested... 98.5 percent of the Armed Forces [didn't] participate in the coup .... Nevertheless, the number

> **Unfortunately for Turkey and the world, Erdoğan used the attempted coup to subvert democracy, which Turks have fought for over 93 years, to achieve increasingly totalitarian goals. Like Putin in Russia, Erdoğan has since sought to create some formal, but shallow, institutions of democracy.**

of staff in the military was (immediately) axed from 561,641 to 351,176. A great majority of (discharged) officers and non-commissioned officers ... have remained behind bars for almost a year without a trial and conviction."

Even before July 15, 2016, Erdoğan's government had prepared lists of public servants to be arrested. A forum on Turkey hosted by the Anatolian Heritage Federation was held within Canada's Parliament in early 2018 where Alex Neve, Secretary General of Amnesty International (AI) Canada, stated that Taner Kılıç, president of AI Turkey, remained in prison for allegedly supporting the so-called "terrorist organization FETÖ" (of Gülen). He added,

[AI] in its 57 years never experienced anything like this before...anyone can be detained and arrested for having a communication app Bylock or sending their child to a Gülen Movement affiliated school or having a bank account in Bank Asya... Turkey [now has] the highest number of jailed journalists...

According to a report issued by UN High Commissioner for Human Rights Zeid Al Hussein:

The numbers are ... staggering: nearly 160,000 people arrested during an 18-month state of emergency; 152,000 civil servants dismissed, many totally arbitrarily; teachers, judges and lawyers dismissed or prosecuted; journalists arrested, media outlets shut down and websites blocked... Turkish authorities reportedly detained some 100 women who were pregnant or ... [new mothers], ... on the grounds that they were 'associates' of their husbands, who are suspected of being connected to terrorist organizations. Some were detained with their children and others violently separated from them. This is ... outrageous, ... cruel, and (has nothing) ... whatsoever to do with making [Turkey]... safer."

Following the events of July 2016, Erdoğan unleashed his campaign to destroy the rule of law and the independence of the judiciary. After judges and prosecutors were arrested and purged under dubious charges, first-instance judges were promoted to the appeals courts, and inexperienced newcomers were appointed as replacements. Consequently, many cases are pushed up to appeals courts, which are overwhelmed.

Fear of prosecution paralyzed both the judiciary and academia. Those branded as Gülenists were penalized repeatedly, shunned by employers, and deprived of their passports. The judiciary lost its independence and became Erdoğan's main weapon to pursue perceived opponents. Judges and prosecutors are held in prisons. Many were dismissed from their positions without a fair process with their assets frozen. They cannot leave Turkey and the Judges and Prosecutors Association (YARSAV) that independently represented them has been administratively disbanded.

The Turkish High Judicial Council (HSYK) failed to serve as a guarantor of the independence of the judiciary in face of the overreaches of power by the State. It became an extension of Erdoğan's authority, either promoting or allowing all abuses being perpetrated. Its suspension on December 8th, 2016 by the European Network of the Councils for the Judiciary (ENCJ) illustrates the disappearance of rule of law across Turkey. >>>

FREEDOM CONVENTION

FREEDOM CONVENTION

With a bare 51.3% of the vote on April 16, 2017, the "Yes" campaign won Turkey's historic referendum on constitutional amendments. Ruling by emergency decree, Erdoğan's government silenced independent media, restricted public debate, and jailed critical journalists and leaders of the pro-Kurdish opposition.

The parliamentary system in Turkey was transformed into an executive presidency: one-man rule. Human dignity, the rule of law, and the judiciary were all threatened when Erdoğan was given the power to appoint ministers, legislate by decree, dissolve and reconstitute parliament, and control judicial appointments. The post of prime minister was abolished and parliamentary oversight of the executive branch of government was weakened. The rule of law was hollowed out; democratic governance was profoundly undermined.

Freedom of the press vanished. Writers and editors critical of the government were fired and replaced by government propagandists. Staff on the few newspapers struggling to remain independent were jailed.

The government insists that Turkey remains a democracy because there are still elections, but while Erdoğan's critics languish in jail and many others live in fear, it's democracy in name only. It's now a crime to insult the president, the flag, the republic, or the nation. Erdoğan's team of lawyers and prosecutors regularly check social media. Police arrive at critics' homes. More than 46,000 people have been prosecuted under this charge. Many lost jobs and were imprisoned.

In 2019, Erdoğan announced reforms that would focus on serving the people, securing an independent judiciary, improving access to justice and shortening the length of trials. For many legal professionals, his words rang hollow.

On January 28, 2020, Turkey underwent its third Universal Periodic Review (UPR) before the United Nations Human Rights Council. The UPR addressed its human

> **Human dignity, the rule of law, and the judiciary were all threatened when Erdoğan was given the power to appoint ministers, legislate by decree, dissolve and reconstitute parliament, and control judicial appointments.**

rights crisis and the dramatic erosion of its rule of law framework, but Erdoğan refused to acknowledge the key issues at the center of the crisis and to commit to addressing the increasing erosion of judicial independence and abusive use of criminal proceedings and detention to target critics. Restrictions on free speech and the media are growing. A systematic failure to investigate abuses committed by state officials, such as torture and ill-treatment in custody, continues.

About 15 million Turkish citizens are caught up in the criminal justice process as witnesses or defendants. There are 7.5 million active criminal cases.

In refusing to accept the UPR's recommendations to introduce a constitutional amendment to make the Council of Judges and Prosecutors independent of the executive, Turkey's justice system will remain under the political control of the presidency and the AKP. The prolonged detention of human rights defenders Osman Kavala and Selahattin Demirtas illustrates the impact of political court decisions along with Turkey's readiness to flout the binding judgments of the European Court of Human Rights.

Turkish citizens deserve to live in a functioning democracy with the rule of law. Erdoğan seems determined to remove all elements of Atatürk's secular state. Turkey's global friends can only hope that he will accept the real lessons of the 2016 events, instead of terming it a "gift from God", and move back towards national reconciliation, democracy and the rule of law. ■

FREEDOM CONVENTION

FREEDOM CONVENTION

Y. ALP ASLANDOĞAN

Dr. Y. Alp Aslandoğan is the Executive Director of the Alliance for Shared Values (AFSV). He previously served as the board president of the Institute of Interfaith Dialog in Houston, Texas. Aslandogan is the co-editor of "Muslim Citizens of the Globalized World: Contributions of the Gulen Movement" and has penned columns for CNN, Huffington Post, and Foxnews.com. He also serves as a contributing editor for the Fountain magazine and on the Board of Scholars and Practitioners of the Journal of Interreligious Dialogue.

It is important to note that the Hizmet movement became a persecuted minority as the primary target of the oppressive regime of president Erdoğan along with journalists and Kurds. With this in mind, I want to briefly touch upon three points: First, the mechanics of the collapse of the rule of law in Turkey; second, what in my view enabled this outcome; and finally the extent of the human rights violations against the Hizmet movement that this collapse facilitated.

MECHANICS OF THE COLLAPSE:

The subjugation of the judiciary and its transformation into a punitive weapon is a core pillar of Erdoğan's strategy of bringing four major power centers under his control; the others being big money, media, and the military.

The Turkish judiciary has suffered from bias and lack of independence throughout the history of the Turkish Republic. However, the blatant instrumentalization of the judiciary in the hands of an elected civilian government which has occurred over the last five years is unprecedented. Mechanically, three stages eventually culminated in the judiciary becoming a punitive political instrument: changing laws, changing court systems, and dominating the high council to manipulate judge appointments.

In stage one, Erdoğan declared the public corruption probes of December 2013 an attempt at a judicial coup by Gülen sympathizers in the judiciary. He declared Gülen and his sympathizers enemies of the state and called for a war on those who, in his rhetoric, attempted to topple the elected government. According to law No. 6524, the justice minister was empowered within the High Council of Judges and Prosecutors (HSYK) to make key appointments. The AKP-dominated parliament then passed laws to make arrests much easier and to consolidate arrest decisions into the hands of a carefully controlled group of judges. Existing laws required search warrants to be issued based on "strong doubt based on concrete evidence" of wrongdoing. The new law No. 6572 adapted in December 2014 made demonstrating reasonable doubt sufficient to get a search warrant.

In June 2014, with law No. 6545, a new system of Special Criminal Judges or Criminal Peace Judgeships was created for criminal investigations which was then abused for political purposes. Instead of arrest warrant decisions being made by a large number of courts spread around the country, those decisions fell to a smaller number of courts with fewer judges.

The final step of the judiciary subjugation was the domination of the HSYK. The constitutional amendment of September 2010 made membership determination of the High Council of Judges and Prosecutors much more democratic. Erdoğan did not have enough loyalists in the judiciary to dominate the High Council elections. He already had an alliance with the MHP nationalists, but he did something nobody expected him to do – he allied with the neo-nationalists.

FACTORS ENABLING THE COLLAPSE:

Erdoğan's clever tactic of targeting big money and the media allowed him to control most media outlets by the time he started his moves to dominate the judiciary. He was therefore able to justify his moves on the judiciary with an enemy rhetoric and scapegoating the Hizmet movement. Another contributing factor was the decades-long "ideology-oriented" practice of the higher judiciary and the constitutional court, as opposed to a "rights-oriented" practice. This led to a significant segment of the population continuing to support AKP in the face of ongoing violations of freedom of expression, corruption, and now the assault on the judiciary. The last enabling factor was the masterful use of "enemy of the state" and "judicial coup" rhetorics by Erdoğan to justify his power grab.

Now I want to talk about the impact of the collapse of rule of law on the Hizmet movement as the primary target of the Erdoğan regime.

IMPACTS OF THE COLLAPSE:

In the aftermath of the horrific attempted coup in July 2016, the Erdoğan government began targeting everybody associated with the Hizmet movement. On March 10, 2020, Turkish interior minister Süleyman Soylu announced that 511,000 people were investigated based on suspicion of being associated with the Hizmet movement, including 379,732 men, 103,517 women and 2,060 minors – over 180,000 were jailed or imprisoned at some point. This is comparable to the U.S. government investigating everyone in Atlanta, and arresting half of them. 30,679 individuals are currently in prison including thousands of women and hundreds of children who are living in prison with their mothers. 1,546 Turkish lawyers have been prosecuted and 598 lawyers have been arrested since >>>

FREEDOM CONVENTION

July 2016, according to a report by Arrested Lawyers, a Europe-based organization advocating for the lawyer victims of Erdoğan's persecution.

Report on the Impact of the State of Emergency on Human Rights in Turkey (by United Nations Office of the High Commissioner for Human Rights, March 2018) estimated that "approximately 600 women with young children were being held in detention in Turkey as of December 2017, including about 100 women who were pregnant or had just given birth." The OHCHR report documented "at least 50 cases of women who had given birth just before or just after being detained or arrested." OHCHR also reported receiving a report "concerning a woman who was sexually assaulted by a police officer during arrest" and "at least six cases of women who were detained while they were visiting their spouses in prison". These women were, according to the OHCHR report, "either detained together with their children or violently separated from them."

> **While I do not argue the Erdoğan government's treatment of the Hizmet movement fulfills the criteria for atrocity crimes under international law, it is striking to see that evidence for several of the 10 stages described by Dr. Stanton can be observed in Turkey against Hizmet participants.**

The United Nations Special Rapporteur on Torture and Other Cruel, Inhumane or Degrading Treatment or Punishment visited Turkey from Nov. 27 to Dec. 2, 2016, and reported that torture was widespread following the failed coup, particularly at the time of arrest and subsequent detention. The number of investigations reportedly carried out into allegations of torture was, in his words, "grossly disproportionate to the alleged frequency of violations." He also reported that the majority of the victims of torture did not file complaints to the authorities for fear of retaliation against them or their families and because of a deep distrust in the independence of the prosecution and the judiciary.

In April of 2017, the Council of Europe Parliamentary Assembly voted to reinstate a full monitoring procedure against Turkey after 13 years, citing "serious concerns" about respect for human rights, democracy, and the rule of law. The European Parliament, on March 13, 2019, voted 370 to 109 to call on the European

countries to formally suspend Turkey's EU accession process. Several governments, including Norway, Germany, The United Kingdom, Canada, and Australia reached the determination that the Hizmet movement became a persecuted minority and the movement participants have a legitimate fear of being persecuted solely due to their association with the movement. Against this universal criticism and condemnation, Turkish government officials are in a mode of denial that gives the impression of living in a parallel universe.

The United Nations considers atrocity crimes as the most serious crimes against humankind. Their status as international crimes is based on the belief that the acts associated with them affect the core dignity of human beings, in particular the persons that should be most protected by states, both in times of peace and in times of war. Atrocity crimes include genocide, crimes against humanity, and war crimes.

Genocide, according to international law, is a crime committed against members of a national, ethnic, racial, or religious group. Even though the victims of the crimes are individuals, they are targeted because of their membership, real or perceived, in one of these groups. Crimes against humanity encompass acts that are part of a widespread or systematic attack directed against any civilian population.

Dr. Gregory Stanton, the President of Genocide Watch defined the 10 stages to genocide as follows:

1. **Classification,**
2. **Symbolization,**
3. **Discrimination,**
4. **Dehumanization,**
5. **Organization,**
6. **Polarization,**
7. **Preparation,**
8. **Persecution,**
9. **Extermination, and**
10. **Denial.**

While I do not argue the Erdoğan government's treatment of the Hizmet movement fulfills the criteria for atrocity crimes under international law, it is striking to see that evidence for several of the 10 stages described by Dr. Stanton can be observed in Turkey against Hizmet participants.

I hope and pray that the situation does not get any worse for the participants of the Hizmet movement, journalists, Kurds, or any other persecuted group. ■

FREEDOM CONVENTION

FREEDOM CONVENTION

KISTEN KRISH GOVENDER

Kisten Krish Govender is a professor at the University of Kwazulu-Natal College of Law and Management Studies in South Africa. He is also an elected member of the Legal Practice Center of South Africa.

THE COLLAPSE OF THE RULE OF LAW IN TURKEY - A SOUTH AFRICAN PERSPECTIVE

A discussion on the importance of upholding the rule of law in Turkey is intertwined with the role and ever-growing powers of the President of Turkey. The greater the power of the President, the weaker the strength of the rule of law – until one extinguishes the other.

Turkey is often seen as the "umbilical cord" between East and West in Europe and is also symbolic of the great North/South and East/West divides within the world. When Constantinople fell in 1453, Turkey became a force that reverberated throughout the centuries thereafter. It impacted world and regional affairs in many ways, some small but more often with significant effect.

The actions of President Erdoğan, having started as a modern and progressive leader, shifted course over two presidential terms in order to deflect attention away from his questionable conduct and his strong critics. Doing so set himself on the path towards a form of modern-day dictatorship whilst strengthening his hold over a weakened and subservient Parliament. Erdoğan thus wields widespread power over the masses of the people via his influence over the army, intelligence, and police services. This could only have been kept in check by a strong and independent judiciary, which sadly does not exist today.

In any modern democracy, the rule of law is balanced by the judiciary, which acts as the guardian of all the rights of the people against potential unjust or unfair actions of the executive and legislative powers, which form the other two arms of the state. The importance of an independent judiciary cannot be emphasized enough in order to ensure strong adherence to the rule of law. Politicians have a somewhat superficial understanding of the role of a judiciary and most times expect the judiciary to interpret and apply the law as it is written and passed by the legislature.

The strength of the judiciary is greatly dependent on the requirements for the appointment and removal of members of the judiciary. The more independent the processes for the appointment and removal of judges, the stronger is the rule of law. The role of the judiciary is crucial in the battle against unjust rule, as it is the last barrier against dictatorships and military rule.

Power hungry or desperate leaders of democratic countries will seek ways to emasculate the judiciary, through different ways. History has shown us the many ways that this has happened, especially over the last century. One method popularly used is a "state of emergency". The events of July 15, 2016, involving a purported coup by a few members of the Turkish army, which at best can be described as "poorly planned", or as others might say, "stage managed" by Erdoğan himself, with tragic consequences for hundreds of people who lost their lives by coming out into the streets, set the stage for the collapse of the rule of law in Turkey.

A then-credible democratic government was turned within days into an authoritarian one. President Erdoğan was able to use emergency powers to usurp the legislative and judicial powers and rule by decree. The Parliament was bypassed and the judiciary was rendered impotent.

A facade of the rule of law remains today in respect of commercial and non political legal matters. However, anyone who is deemed to be an opponent not necessarily of the State, but of Erdoğan and his pliant Government, can and will be arrested and detained, and often with assaults and torture to follow. If they are fortunate to survive the ordeal of detention, they will be charged under draconian and unjust laws as decreed by the State. When they are brought to Court to be prosecuted, their convictions are a matter of formality and the sentences are severe.

>>>

> "Turkey, like all other oppressive regimes, exists within a new world order underpinned by the rise of unilateralism, nationalism, religious factionalism, ethnicity, racism, tribalism, subjugation of minorities, violence against women, excesses of the mining industry, and the irreversible environmental destruction of Mother Earth."

FREEDOM CONVENTION

FREEDOM CONVENTION

The judiciary has become a partner of this tyranny, giving Turkey a false sense of adhering to the rule of law.

How, in this electronic age of free-flowing information via social media and numerous networks, can false news, misinformation and lies be so strongly advocated and promoted, thereby enabling dictators, mass murderers, and tyrants to perpetuate unjust rule with impunity? Turkey cannot be separated from the global realities and geopolitical forces that pose an existential threat to almost every inhabitant of this world. Unfortunately, Turkey is also mired in a murky world of warfare and underworld of political intrigue, kidnappings, assassinations, and disappearances.

Turkey, like all other oppressive regimes, exists within a new world order underpinned by the rise of unilateralism, nationalism, religious factionalism, ethnicity, racism, tribalism, subjugation of minorities, violence against women, excesses of the mining industry, and the irreversible environmental destruction of Mother Earth. Seen alongside the many other forms of discrimination and class oppression faced by the poor and dispossessed throughout many parts of the world and the consequences of pandemics, climate change and the dark cyber world of artificial intelligence, Turkey can pretend to be better than many. These are the signs of human failure on a monumental global level. Thus, under this ominous global cloud of doom, Erdoğan has been able to pursue, and justify, his grandiose dreams of world leadership.

As an aside, let me say that South Africa, my great country, offered a beacon of hope to the world by transitioning peacefully, under the leadership of great visionaries Oliver Tambo and Nelson Mandela, away from one of humanity's worst oppressive systems.

Only the brave people of Turkey can reverse this oppressive tide, restore the rule of law for all its people, and regain legitimacy in the eyes of the world as a truly great nation achieving success and prosperity in a non-sectarian and just manner. The good people of the world, no matter how small in number, will stand with all those in exile, in prison and outside prison, fighting for justice, peace, prosperity and unity for all in Turkey. ■

JAMES HARRINGTON

> Jim Harrington, a human rights attorney of forty-five years, is founder and director emeritus of the Texas Civil Rights Project. He graduated from the University of Detroit law school in 1973, from where he also holds a master's in philosophy. He was an adjunct professor at the University of Texas law school for 27 years and also taught undergraduate writing courses in civil liberties. By the time of his retirement in March 2016, he had built the Project to a staff of 40 people with offices in Austin, El Paso, South Texas, Houston, Dallas, and Odessa.

What we see in Turkey is a reflection of what's going on around the world. We are experiencing a similar struggle in the U.S. with Trump right now and perhaps the thing that's going to save us is the judiciary. The judiciary is of course theoretically essential to the safe functioning of any democracy, because it divides power. Concerning the attack on the judiciary in Turkey, it seems that Trump and Erdoğan use the same language about enemies of the people. Both are demagogues. What I believe is different is that the United States has had 250 years to do to build and protect the autonomy of the judiciary. Though it is imperfect, it is a longstanding part of American tradition and the American people see its autonomy from the executive branch as essential.

Turkey, on the other hand, has only really had 10 years of experience with an independent judiciary and not enough time for it to become institutionalized. Historically in Turkey, up until probably around 2000, the judiciary was nothing but a rubber stamp for the government and was complicit in the government's torture and abuse of human rights. THings changed in 2002, during that bright decade when it looked like Turkey was reforming and coming around as a human rights leader, establishing democracy in the Middle East. When President Obama was elected, Turkey was the first country he visited because of that promise of change in the fledgling democracy. So in that bright decade, there was a very considerable effort to reform and strengthen the judiciary and to make it independent. >>>

FREEDOM CONVENTION

FREEDOM CONVENTION

Turkey was making these moves, to some extent, to join the EU, and the EU involved itself significantly through both education and financial support in order to aid in the creation of an independent judiciary in Turkey. The goal that the EU embarked upon was training 10,000 lawyers and judges in the tradition of becoming independent, becoming a check on the executive and legislative power. I wrote a book on the Fethullah Gülen trials in Turkey and in the process, I looked very closely at the judicial system and how it functioned. Part of the process of writing that book was interviewing judges and prosecutors in Turkey, which I did with judges on both the trial level and with the judges of the Constitutional Court. What was striking to me was their dedication and interest in really forming an independent judiciary, really bringing about this hope in Turkey to build a democracy in which the judiciary played an important role in curtailing power and protecting human rights.

There were constitutional amendments in 2007 that were very important to this process, that strengthened human rights and civil liberties in the Turkish constitution significantly. Turkey, it's important to note, had voluntarily assented to the jurisdiction of the European Court of Human Rights (ECtHR). When decisions came down against Turkey from the ECtHR, Turkey abided by them during this period. The most important constitutional changes were in 2010. These amendments were very significant in terms of concretely prioritizing human rights in the constitution of Turkey. Then came 2016, and probably at this point, Erdoğan had come to truly understand the danger that these constitutional amendments and being subject to the ECtHR presented to his power. He dramatically clamped down on the courts, putting judges in jail when they made decisions with which he did not agree. Erdoğan fired at least 4,000 judges and sidelined all sorts of people involved in the judicial system, including the prosecutors. He set up courts that are basically what we would call kangaroo courts, putting people in jail whom Erdoğan perceived to be enemies. This list of people throughout Turkey who lost their jobs and were thrown in prison has nothing to do with crime. The common denominator is that they were against Erdoağan's consolidation of power and money.

So, now we have the 2017 constitutional amendments that barely passed. These 27 amendments watered down the constitution as it was amended in 2010. What Erdoğan did in the 2017 amendments was consolidate the size of the independent council and give himself more appointment powers. Essentially Erdoğan and his party now appoint the majority of that council which in turn appoints the judges. This move stripped away any attempt to move to an independent judiciary and made sure that everybody who was selected were nothing more than Erdoğan's cronies. The effect of the 2017 amendments has been to thoroughly destroy any independence in the judiciary, essentially turning back the clock to the judiciary that existed prior to 2000. The judiciary will now implement anything that Erdoğan wants.

The real tragedy experienced by ordinary Turkish citizens is that the vast majority of cases do not involve the political whims of Erdoğan. Given the way he has gutted the judiciary and demoralized the judiciary and put in new appointments, the vast majority of these new appointments are very young lawyers, barely out of law school. They're neophytes. They have no idea what it's like to go through trial processes and all of a sudden they're judges. So not only do the people who litigate in these courts face incompetence, which undermines the quality of civil justice, but they also know that they're not independent and that every decision they make has to be approved by the government. The judiciary is in a really sad situation. It's very unfortunate because there were so many years of promise. I hope that when Turkey returns to that long, hard path to democracy, the memory of these ten years will be essential in reforming Turkey.

Having said that, and in the interest of wrapping this up, what's happening in Turkey is not atypical of what's going on around the world right now. In this lack of respect for an independent judiciary, not just lack of respect but the concerted effort to undermine this democratic institution, democratic ideals that we have had for hundreds of years now are being undermined. I think it's important for everybody to stand up and support the efforts of the people in Turkey. I'm reminded of a quote from Robert Kennedy when he was running for president. He went to South Africa back in the days of Apartheid and in those days of Apartheid, of course, the universities were segregated. It meant that he had to choose between a white university and a black university to deliver a speech. So what Kennedy did is he chose to speak at a White university in Durban. He did that because he understood that it was going to have to be the white people in power that brought about change. Talking to the students, he made an important pronouncement that I would like to share. This comes from the speech that he gave at the University of Cape Town on June 6, 1966. "A third danger is timidity. Few men are willing to brave the disapproval of their fellows, the

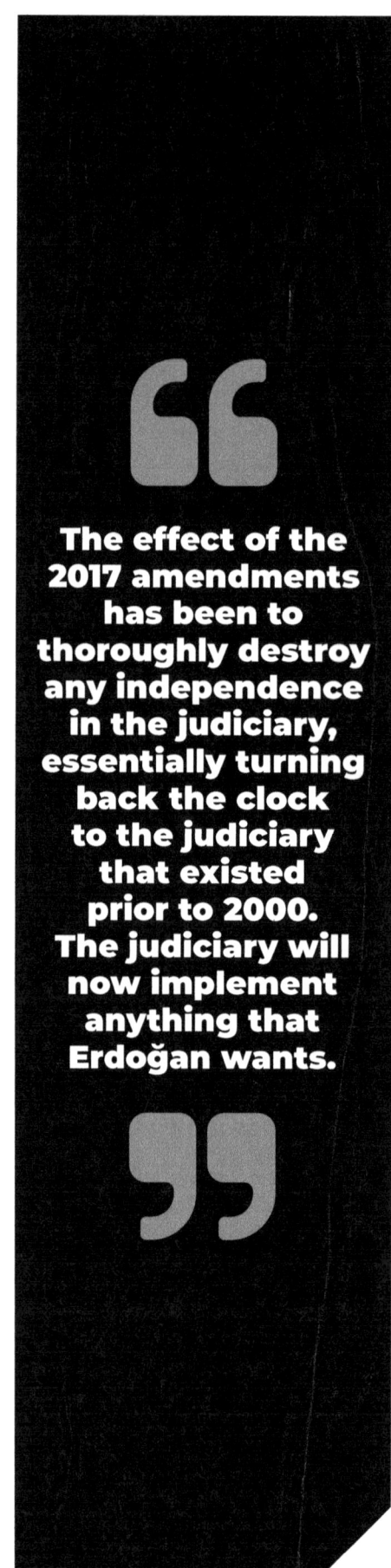

> The effect of the 2017 amendments has been to thoroughly destroy any independence in the judiciary, essentially turning back the clock to the judiciary that existed prior to 2000. The judiciary will now implement anything that Erdoğan wants.

FREEDOM CONVENTION

FREEDOM CONVENTION

censure of their colleagues, the wrath of their society. Moral courage is a rarer commodity than bravery in battle or great intelligence. Yet it is the one essential, vital quality for those who seek to change the world which yields most painfully to change. Aristotle tells us "At the Olympic games it is not the finest or the strongest men who are crowned, but those who enter the lists... so too in the life of the honorable and the good it is they who act rightly who win the prize." I believe that in this generation those with the courage to enter the conflict will find themselves with companions in every corner of the world."

SHIFT FROM DEMOCRATIZATION TOWARDS AUTHORITARIANISM IN TURKEY:
THE RISE OF POLITICAL ISLAM

FREEDOM CONVENTION

ALON BEN MEIR

> Dr. Alon Ben Meir is a professor and Senior Fellow at New York University's Center for Global Affairs and Senior Fellow at the World Policy Institute. Ben-Meir is an expert on Middle East politics and affairs, specializing in international negotiations and conflict resolution. In the past two decades, Ben-Meir has been directly involved in various backchannel negotiations involving Israel and its neighboring countries and Turkey. Ben-Meir holds a master's degree in philosophy and a doctorate in international relations from Oxford University.

TURKEY'S SHIFT FROM DEMOCRACY TO AUTHORITARIANISM

Turkey's President Erdoğan is becoming ever more dangerous as he continues to ravage his own country and destabilize scores of states in the Middle East, the Balkans, and North Africa, while cozying up to Russia's Putin, the West's foremost adversary. Sadly, there seems to be no appetite for most EU member states to challenge Erdoğan and put him on notice that he can no longer pursue his authoritarianism while destroying what's left of Turkey's democracy, alongside his adventurous meddling abroad with impunity.

To understand the severity of Erdoğan's actions and ambitions and their dire implications, it suffices to quote Ahmet Davutoglu, formerly one of Erdoğan's closest associates who served as Minister of Foreign Affairs and subsequently Prime Minister. Following his forced resignation in May 2016 he stated "I will sustain my faithful relationship with our president until my last breath. No one has ever heard — and will ever hear — a single word against our president come from my mouth."

Yet on October 12, Davutoglu declared "Erdoğan left his friends who struggled and fought with him in exchange for the symbols of ancient Turkey, and he is trying to hold us back now.... You yourself [Erdoğan] are the calamity. The biggest calamity that befell these people is the regime that turned the country into a disastrous family business."

The stunning departure of Davutoglu from his earlier statement shows how desperate conditions have become, and echoed how far and how dangerously

Erdoğan has gone. Erdoğan has inflicted a great calamity on his own people, and his blind ambition outside Turkey is destabilizing many countries while dangerously undermining Turkey and its Western allies' national security and strategic interests.

A brief synopsis of Erdoğan's criminal domestic practices and his foreign misadventures tell the whole story. Domestically, he incarcerated tens of thousands of innocent citizens on bogus charges, including hundreds of journalists. Meanwhile, he is pressuring the courts to send people to prison for insulting him. No one can even express their thoughts about this ruthlessness, which is an egregious violation of democratic norms. Internationally, Erdoğan ordered Turkish intelligence operatives to kill or smuggle back to the country Turkish citizens affiliated with the Gülen movement.

He regularly cracks down on Turkey's Kurdish minority, preventing them from living a normal life in accordance with their culture, language, and traditions, even though they have been and continue to be loyal Turkish citizens. There is no solution to the conflict except a political one, as former Foreign Minister Ali Babacan adamantly stated on October 20: "a solution [to the Kurdish issue] will be political and we will defend democracy persistently." This of course sadly remains beyond the capabilities of any pro-democracy activists as long as Erdoğan is still in power.

Erdoğan refuses to accept the Law of the Sea convention that gives countries, including Cyprus, the right to an Exclusive Economic Zone (EEZ) for energy exploration while threatening the use of force against Greece, another NATO member no less. He openly sent a research ship to the region for oil and gas deposits, which EU foreign policy chief Josep Borrell called "extremely worrying." This shows how little respect he pays to NATO's charter that enshrines democratic principles, which he has been defying with impunity.

He invaded Syria with Trump's blessing to prevent the Syrian Kurds from establishing autonomous rule, under the pretext of fighting the PKK and the YPG (the Syrian Kurdish militia that fought side-by-side the US, and whom Erdoğan falsely accuses of being a terrorist group).

He is sending weapons to the Sunni in northern Lebanon while setting up a branch of the Turkish Cooperation and Coordination Agency (TIKA) in the country—a practice Erdoğan has used often to gain a broader foothold in countries where it has an interest, wholly in line with his authoritarian leanings.

While the Turkish economy is in tatters, he is investing hundreds of millions of dollars in the Balkans, flooding countries with Turkish imams to spread his Islamic gospel and to ensure their place in his neo-Ottoman orbit while neglecting the more than 20 million Turks who are living in abject poverty. Criticizing Erdoğan's economic leadership, Babacan put it succinctly when he said this month that "It is not possible in Turkey for the economic or financial system to continue, or political legitimacy hold up."

Erdoğan is corrupt to the bone. He conveniently appointed his son-in-law as Finance Minister, which allows him to hoard tens of millions of dollars, as Davutoğlu slyly pointed out: >>>

FREEDOM CONVENTION

FREEDOM CONVENTION

"The only accusation against me...is the transfer of land to an educational institution over which I have no personal rights and which I cannot leave to my daughter, my son, my son-in-law or my daughter-in-law."

Erdoğan is backing Azerbaijan in its dispute with Armenia (backed by Iran) over the breakaway territory of Nagorno-Karabakh, which is inhabited by ethnic Armenians and has been the subject of dispute for over 30 years. This is a part of Erdoğan's continuing vindictiveness against Armenians, which is a gross violation of international law to which a despot like Erdoğan pays no heed.

He is exploiting Libya's civil strife by providing the Government of National Accord (GNA) with drones and military equipment to help Tripoli gain the upper hand in its battle against Khalifa Haftar's forces. Former Foreign Minister Yaşar Yakış said in February 2020 that "The unclear Turkish foreign policy by Erdoğan may put Turkey in grave danger due to this expansion towards Libya."

He is meddling in the Israeli-Palestinian conflict to prevent them from settling their dispute unless Israel meets Palestinian demands. He granted several Hamas officials Turkish citizenship to spite Israel, even though Hamas openly calls for Israel's destruction.

He betrayed NATO by buying the Russian-made S-400 air defense system, which seriously compromises the alliance's technology and intelligence.

He is destabilizing many countries, including Somalia, Qatar, Libya, and Syria, by dispatching military forces and hardware while violating the air space of other countries like Iraq, Cyprus, and Greece. Yakis said Turkey is engaging in a "highly daring bet where the risks of failure are enormous."

Erdoğan supports extremist Islamist groups such as the Muslim Brotherhood and Hamas, and an assortment of jihadists, including ISIS, knowing full well that these groups are sworn enemies of the West—yet he uses them as a tool to promote his wicked Islamic agenda.

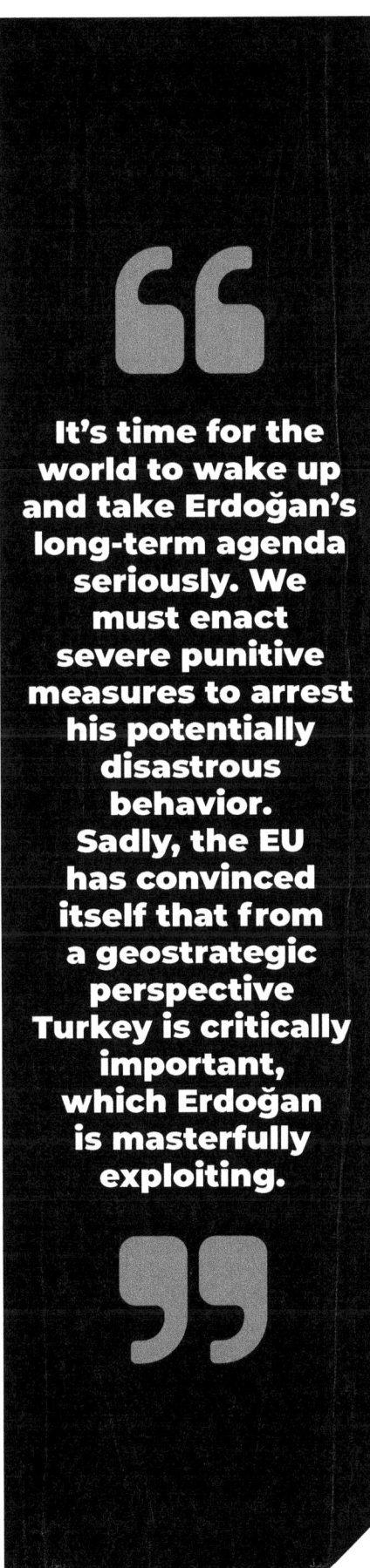

> It's time for the world to wake up and take Erdoğan's long-term agenda seriously. We must enact severe punitive measures to arrest his potentially disastrous behavior. Sadly, the EU has convinced itself that from a geostrategic perspective Turkey is critically important, which Erdoğan is masterfully exploiting.

He regularly blackmails EU members, threatening to flood Europe with Syrian refugees unless they support his foreign escapades such as his invasion of Syria, and provide him with billions in financial aid to cope with the Syrian refugees.

The question is, how much more evidence do the EU and UN need to act? A close look at Erdoğan's conduct illuminates his ultimate ambition to restore much of the Ottoman Empire's influence over the countries that were once under its control, imposing his authoritarian whims on the broader region, akin to sultans in the heyday of the Ottoman Empire.

Erdoğan is dangerous. He has cited Hitler as an example of an effective executive presidential system and may seek to acquire nuclear weapons. It's time for the world to wake up and take Erdoğan's long-term agenda seriously. We must enact severe punitive measures to arrest his potentially disastrous behavior. Sadly, the EU has convinced itself that from a geostrategic perspective Turkey is critically important, which Erdoğan is masterfully exploiting.

The EU must be prepared to take a stand against Erdoğan, with or without the U.S. Let's hope, though, that President-Elect Joe Biden together with the EU will warn Erdoğan that his days of authoritarianism and foreign adventurism are over.

FREEDOM CONVENTION

BÜLENT KENEŞ

Bulent Kenes, PhD, is an exiled Turkish journalist and academician. He authored 7 books on topics of Iran, Islam, Turkish politics, and human rights. Keneş, who has over 25 years of experience in journalism, was the founding editor-in-chief of Today's Zaman daily. He was also among the founders of Stockholm Center for Freedom (SCF). He is now a member of a team establishing the European Center for Populism Studies (ECPS) based in Brussels.

As it is well-known, all Islamists are Muslim, but not all Muslims are Islamists. This simple logic, which is applicable throughout the Islamic world, is true of Turkey as well. The story of political Islamism in Turkey, which built its power on the exploitation of religious fervor, has turned over time into a hatred of secularism and diversity in general.

By polarising society, political Islamists have increasingly guided Turkey's social and political discourse towards discrimination and hate, overshadowing the peaceful messages of Islam. For much of its history, Turkey has been largely devoid of Islamism, but political Islam has now been imported from Pakistan, Egypt, and North Africa where it was developed as a reaction against colonialism. It is not difficult to see that the Muslim Brotherhood in Egypt and Jamaat-i Islami in Pakistan gave birth to the political Islamism on which Erdoğan's regime is built.

However, following the 1979 Iranian Revolution, the influence of Iranian Islamism became more dominant over Turkish political Islamists. The agenda of Erdoğan's political mentor, Necmettin Erbakan, was based on Islamist ideas that were radicalized by anti-colonialist movements and a revolutionary mentality predominant in Iran rather than the moderate local religious concepts of Turkey. Most books and other materials that significantly influenced Turkish political Islamists were generally Turkish translations of works published by radicalized Islamist groups outside of Turkey.

Against such a background, Erdoğan established the Justice and Development Party (AKP) with a group of associates in 2001 and publicly declared that he was maintaining his distance from Islamism, saying "I have taken off the shirt of Milli Görüş [or National View]." The party program and election manifestos were consistent with democratic reformist commitments in support of Erdoğan's "I have changed" discourse.

Indeed, the AKP and Erdoğan began to fulfill their commitments to rapid democratization of the state, unification of Turkish society, and integration of Turkey with the Western world during their first years in power. Thus, they gained a positive reputation and credibility both at home and abroad. The Gülen movement, with its rich human capital, civil society entities, and media engagement fully supported AKP's democratization policies and reform, which reshapedTurkish society with the goal of membership in the European Union.

The democratic and social reforms released by Erdoğan and his AKP eventually rose to a fifty percent approval rate within Turkey. Throughout the struggle against the anti-democratic structures, not only was the dominant military tutelage broken but also a strong pro-Erdoğan media and general societal sentiment were created.

After seeing fifty percent of the popular vote cast for the AKP in the 2011 elections, in which his party ran on the promise to draft a new democratic constitution, Erdoğan had a great opportunity before him. Instead of using this opportunity to fulfill the commitments he had made before the elections, Erdoğan returned to his ideological factory settings: his controversial, radical political Islamist origins.

The Arab revolts that erupted in early 2011 added an imperialist agenda into the mix. Erdoğan used proxy groups and organizations to influence political developments in several neighboring countries. In Syria, since he could not cover the cost of his illegitimate activities with legitimate public funds, he used bribery and laundered dirty money from illegal oil trade conducted by Iran, which was under UN sanctions.

Erdoğan was not only caught up in this dirty business, he also expected all segments of society, including the Gülen movement, to support these illegitimate initiatives. Erdoğan was finally first exposed to the world when a corruption and bribery scandal exploded in December 2013 and then when trucks belonging to the Turkish National Intelligence Organization (MİT) were discovered carrying weapons to radical Islamist terrorist organizations in Syria in early 2014.

Contrary to Erdoğan's expectations, the Gülen movement started to distance itself from Erdoğan and his AKP. This distance increased as the AKP and Erdoğan moved further and further from the ideals of democracy they once touted. Because of this divergence, Erdoğan launched a witch-hunt to annihilate the Gülen movement.

Erdoğan has argued that his exposure in December of 2013 was an attempted "coup" to topple his government, contrary to the abundance of evidence displaying his corruption and bribery. He claimed the illegal operations were carried out by police, prosecutors >>>

FREEDOM CONVENTION

and judges who were close to the Gülen movement, and he set out to tear down state mechanisms and the judiciary. He also launched an intense, systematic, and widespread campaign of hatred to discredit the Gulen movement.

Unfortunately, his efforts began by shutting down all media which opposed him; very quickly Erdoğan became the only influential voice in Turkish society. In spite of all this, he could not fully convince Turkey or the world of the unfounded arguments he put forward against the Gülen movement so he devised a conspiracy in July 2016 in which he attempted to achieve his ultimate objectives as a "gift by God."

Turkey has suffered a loss of reputation and failure in every sense as Erdoğan has continued his unlawful, immoral, and arbitrary persecutions, and systematic human rights violations. Turkey's prestige and credibility have been devastated along with all its democratic institutions and principles.

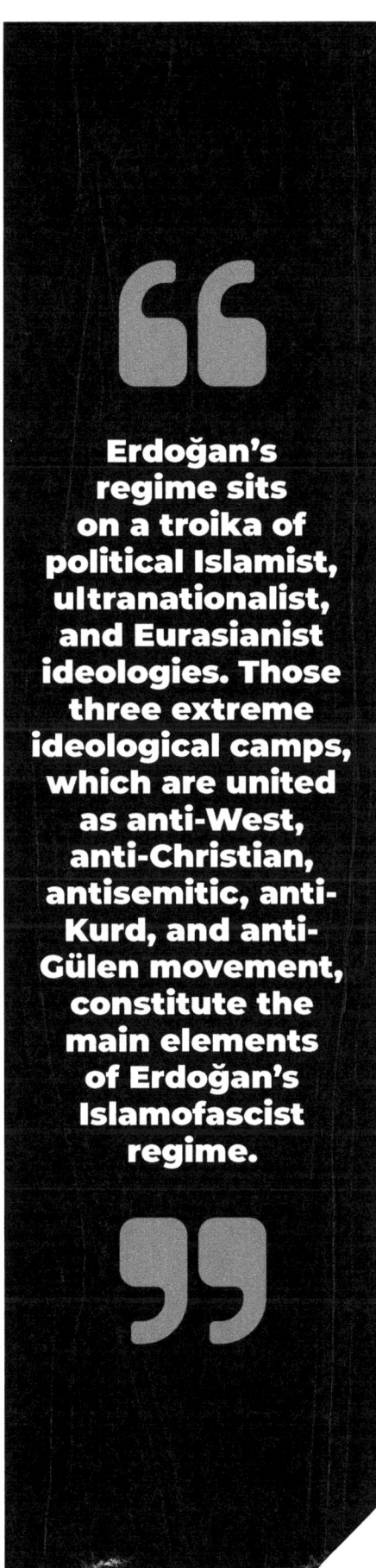

> Erdoğan's regime sits on a troika of political Islamist, ultranationalist, and Eurasianist ideologies. Those three extreme ideological camps, which are united as anti-West, anti-Christian, antisemitic, anti-Kurd, and anti-Gülen movement, constitute the main elements of Erdoğan's Islamofascist regime.

After the Gülen movement distanced itself from him, Erdoğan first tried to ally himself with the Kurdish political movement in order to accumulate more popular power. However, following the corruption scandal in 2013, he desperately needed to search for new partners who had more influence in the judiciary, the military, and the state bureaucracy. So, he tried to find the support he needed from the traditional ultra-nationalists, neo-nationalists, and Eurasianists with their presence in the bureaucracy, army, judiciary, civil society, and the media in order to destroy both the Kurdish political movement and the Gülen movement.

Erdoğan established a pragmatic alliance and an ideological synthesis with these circles, which have racist and fascist leanings. Now Erdoğan's regime sits on a troika of political Islamist, ultranationalist, and Eurasianist ideologies. Those three extreme ideological camps, which are united as anti-West, anti-Christian, antisemitic, anti-Kurd, and anti-Gülen movement, constitute the main elements of Erdoğan's Islamofascist regime. Built upon a foundation of these three toxic ideological elements, a lethal, oppressive regime has ruthlessly hunted those who are not part of this ideal society.

These three poisonous pillars of Erdoğan's Islamofascist regime glorify death and state-sanctioned murder. They radicalize the least educated and informed in Turkish society with appeals based on fear and the twisting of religious and national zeal. After the transformation of the Turkish political system to one-man-rule under the name of the so-called Presidential System, I have analyzed the Erdoğan regime by looking at the well-accepted criteria for dictatorships and I have concluded that Erdoğan's Islamofascist regime is without a doubt a dictatorship.

So, the question here is not whether or not this regime is a dictatorship, but what kind of dictatorship it is. As I understand it, the Erdoğan regime is an authoritarian dictatorship, on the edge of being a totalitarian one. On the one hand, as a full-fledged authoritarian dictatorship, it is normal to see Erdoğan's Islamofascist regime purge about 160,000 public officials from their jobs. BUT it is not normal to see a silent international community and organizations simply sit by and watch these huge persecutions take place.

As a full-fledged authoritarian dictatorship, it is also normal to see Erdoğan's Islamofascist regime detain over 500,000 innocent people and arrest tens of thousands of them. But it is not normal to see an almost silent international community and organizations simply sit by and watch these huge persecutions.

As a full-fledged authoritarian dictatorship, it is normal to see Erdoğan's Islamofascist regime shut down more than 200 media outlets and jail hundreds of dissenting journalists. But it is not normal to see an almost silent international community and organizations simply sit by and watch these huge persecutions.

As a full-fledged authoritarian dictatorship, again, it is normal to see Erdoğan's Islamofascist regime jail thousands of innocent women and hundreds of babies and children. But it is not normal to see an almost silent international community and organizations simply sit by and watch these huge persecutions.

As a full-fledged authoritarian dictatorship, it is normal to see Erdoğan's Islamofascist regime seize all the companies and properties of the members of the Gulen movement and not allow them to find new jobs or establish new businesses and push them to a civil death. But it is not normal to see an almost silent international community and organizations simply sit by and watch these huge persecutions.

As a full-fledged authoritarian dictatorship, it is normal to see Erdoğan's Islamofascist regime seize almost all Kurdish municipalities and to arrest the elected Kurdish mayors and prominent Kurdish politicians. But it is not normal to see an almost silent international community and organizations simply sit by and watch huge persecutions.

As a full-fledged authoritarian dictatorship, it is so normal to see >>>

FREEDOM CONVENTION

FREEDOM CONVENTION

Erdoğan's Islamofascist regime kidnap, torture, and extrajudicially kill those who are allegedly affiliated with the Gülen movement or the members of the Kurdish political movement and other opposition groups. But it is not normal to see an almost silent international community and organizations simply sit by and watch these huge persecutions.

I could list here many more massive persecutions conducted by Erdoğan's Islamofascist regime, but I think these are enough to understand the severity of the situation in Turkey. If any readers would like to learn more about the persecutions under the rule of the Erdoğan regime they could look at my recently published book "A Genocide in the Making".

In conclusion, I would like to underline that Erdoğan's Islamofascist regime has done what is expected from a full-fledged authoritarian dictatorship. No more, no less...

But, the weak-to-non-reaction from the international community and organizations has been a huge disappointment and a real frustration for the victims and persecuted people in Turkey.

So, I would like to make a call to all: Please STOP(!) appeasing Erdoğan's Islamofascist authoritarian dictatorship. Respond to the reality of what Erdoğan's regime is. No more, no less... ■

RABIA CHAUDRY

Rabia Chaudry is an attorney, best-selling author, and advocate. Formerly an International Security Fellow with the U.S. Institute of Peace, Rabia developed and led an international research project on religion and extremism, measuring the ideological attitudes of students in Pakistan and Sri Lanka.

I am an American Muslim, advocate, and activist who has spent seven years watching the growing influence of the Turkish government over American Muslim organizations and leaders in horror.

First, allow me to lay the foundation of Erdoğans ideas in the American Muslim psyche. I think on a global scale it's important to understand why he has been successful in terms of exerting influence over American Muslim organizations and leaders. When Erdoğan first emerged on the international scene, he quickly took on a kind of mythology. The narrative around him was of this strong Muslim leader in an absolute desert of Muslim leadership. But, not just a Muslim leader, an Islamic leader. He was viewed as a resurrector of Islam in Turkey and someone firmly against Israel, where Arab leadership was more compliant in some ways. This is how he reached mythical status in the global Muslim psyche and certainly amongst American Muslims.

So, when the tide began to change in terms of his governance, I don't think many of our communities here were aware. He was hailed as somebody akin to a khalif in the global Muslim community. I became aware of the Turkish government breach in 2016, just a few months after the failed coup. I was attending the annual Islamic Society of North America (ISNA) conference and when the foreign minister of Turkey was given the stage I knew something was wrong. Outside, there were lines of tables piled high with thick books describing the coup. They were being given out to everyone. The government gave away pages and pages of propaganda to extend their reach to all the attendees of ISNA. These colorful books painted Erdoğan as the upholder of the rule of law and democracy who was able to curtail this coup thankfully. I was alarmed by this, I tweeted on social media, >>>

FREEDOM CONVENTION

FREEDOM CONVENTION

saying "what is happening, I've never seen anything like this take place at a domestic conference."

But again, as this is happening, their audience is the average American Muslim who might not be very aware of what's happening politically in other parts of the world and certainly not what's happening on the human rights front in democracy in Turkey.

Since then, there has been a much more concerted effort to groom Muslim leaders, organizations, and communities. About a year ago, Ahmet Yayla issued a report called "Erdoğan's Long Arm in the US." This 200-page document described how his government managed to influence and groom American Muslim organizations. These organizations became platforms to host delegates and are now intertwined with the Turkish government, even though they are domestic American organizations. They have themselves become guests of the Turkish government. Organizations, individuals, and communities have been groomed using invitations for sponsored tourism trips and international conferences held in Turkey. Members of these organizations are invited to very high-level state events and seated at tables with heads of state. They are receiving unreported funding as leaders of American domestic organizations and are well outside of their mandate; this is problematic on an ethical and legal front. Then there's Erdoğan's meddling in the life of local religious institutions. The Turkish government has taken over many different religious establishments and organizations around the country and is also building new ones.

When it comes to human rights violations, the rule of law, and democracy in Turkey there is dead silence from the American Muslim community. You never hear about it and it does not make the news. You have the blacklisting of critics like NBA player Enes Kanter, who was holding a series of basketball camps for young people around the country. In a number of different places, mosques were sponsoring these

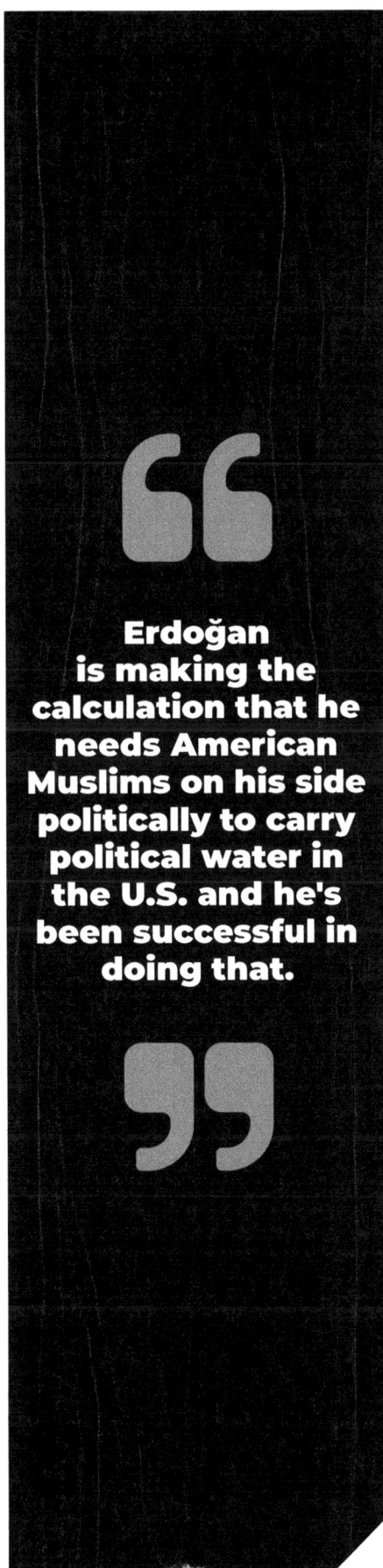

> Erdoğan is making the calculation that he needs American Muslims on his side politically to carry political water in the U.S. and he's been successful in doing that.

basketball camps for young Muslims and other kids in the community. They were pressured by the Turkish consulate and by Turkish officials to cancel these camps and were successful in a number of places.

Erdoğan is making the calculation that he needs American Muslims on his side politically to carry political water in the U.S. and he's been successful in doing that. I would say the only saving grace, ironically, is that American Muslims don't have the kind of political influence that the Turkish government might hope for. At this point, we really cannot sway elections. I would say and I'm grateful that we don't have that power right now, given the attempts to manipulate that power. But, it doesn't mean that there aren't young people in this country being groomed by foreign governments' influences to take leadership positions. I don't know what the long game is but it's problematic that American Muslim organizations don't see the danger in this. They have either deliberately or inadvertently become vehicles for foreign propaganda. I am an opponent of the interference or influence of any government, domestic or foreign, on any domestic organization. It just shouldn't happen. It's not only Turkey, of course, but Turkey's government is already engaged in the systematic crackdown on human rights and democracy on top of the government's influence. But I would hold firm on this for any government, including the American government, should not influence American nonprofits and American Muslim leadership.

My real concern is that these organizations are vital to the institutional life of American Muslims. There is no replacement for them. I must stress that aligning with a foreign government is never a good idea. By allowing this kind of influence to take place they really are compromising the security and future of their own organizations and communities. The political winds can shift at any time and they could be left vulnerable to charges of guilt by association. Because relationships change on an international level, there's no place for the involvement of the government with these kinds of institutions. Our community needs these organizations. I want these organizations to be protected and I want the leaders who have been silent on this or praised the Turkish government for their commitment to human rights and democracy, which is laughable. ■

FREEDOM CONVENTION

FREEDOM CONVENTION

POWER, POLITICAL VIOLENCE, AND VIOLATIONS OF MINORITY RIGHTS IN TURKEY

SÜMEYYE AVCI

Sümeyye Avcı, who worked as a teacher until she was dismissed by the Decree No. 672 in 2016, struggled to survive under social pressure and official restrictions with her husband, who was exposed to similar difficulties. While she is trying to make a living as a photographer, she is fighting for the rights of similarly persecuted citizens as part of the Union Union of the Platforms for KHK Victims.

I would like to talk about the imprisoned women and children who were victims of the so-called 15 July 2016 coup attempt. These are ordinary women who worked in public institutions or bodies of the state; served as academics and hardworking housewives; and are mothers, sisters, daughters, and humans.

These women were accused of using an app called ByLock or depositing money in a private bank called Bank Asya. This bank was targeted by the Turkish government for its connection to the Hizmet movement and was later seized. Again, accusations included being a member of trade unions connected to the Gülen movement, and being a relative of those dismissed by statutory decrees. These women were also accused of organizing or participating in charity sales to help the people in need.

With no criminal investigation against these women, they have been declared members of a terrorist organization overnight. Their basic citizenship rights were stripped away one by one.

Women working in private schools, preparatory courses, and similar institutions were accused of being terrorist organizations for nothing more than participating in educational activities and devoted their lives to education. These schools and institutions operated under the permission and control of the Ministry of National Education and were suddenly defined as places operating against the state. Those working in these educational institutions were subjected to social isolation. Their licenses and diplomas were revoked. They were no longer allowed to work anywhere else. It was declared illegal to do what they loved. >>>

FREEDOM CONVENTION

FREEDOM CONVENTION

Some of these women were subjected to social genocide without a sliver of evidence that they had participated in any acts of violence. Some of them were acquitted at the end of the trials, but others were sentenced anywhere from 3 months to 7 years in prison. They came from all backgrounds; some women were pregnant, had small children, recently married, or had older children when sentenced and sent away. Many of these qualified women could not find a job afterward. Some try to earn their living by selling things in local markets, and some by selling products they make at home on social media. Some of them spend their lives in Turkish prisons.

Life has become even more difficult for women whose husbands are in prison. They have to take care of their husbands in prison, their children, and survive in the face of financial difficulties. Many women cannot overcome their traumas and spend their lives like a nightmare.

This genocide forced women with their children and babies in their arms to cross the Maritsa River or the Aegean Sea for freedom. Dozens of women and children lost their lives while crossing rivers and seas to escape the regime's oppression. These are just a few names lost in this massive tragedy: all members of the Maden family lost their lives; Hatice Akçabay and Ayşe Abdurrezzak passed away with their three children; Esma Uludağ was lucky to have crossed the river with her three children, but she died in Greece from a heart attack despite her young age. Another, Halime Gülsu, died in prison because her medicines were not given to her. As in many similar cases, Montenegro, who was expected to be released from prison but was taken back to prison. They added more charges just to keep him in jail.

Thousands of women like them are deprived of the most basic rights necessary for a humane life in prisons. They are even deprived of the basic right to health. Even at the height of the COVID-19 pandemic, their condition was dire.

We want justice for human rights violations.

> **This genocide forced women with their children and babies in their arms to cross the Maritsa River or the Aegean Sea for freedom. Dozens of women and children lost their lives while crossing rivers and seas to escape the regime's oppression.**

MICHAEL RUBIN

Michael Rubin is a resident scholar at the American Enterprise Institute in Washington, DC, and a senior lecturer at the Naval Postgraduate School in Monterey, California. He has testified on Turkey and other topics both in the U.S. Congress and Australian parliament, and is the author of several books, and more than one thousand op-eds regarding the Middle East.

The core purpose of diplomacy is not only conflict resolution but also conflict avoidance. Where diplomacy often goes wrong, however, is when the desire to avoid conflict results in ascribing reality to an illusion. When diplomats calibrate policy to what they wish reality would be rather than what it is, they may win short-term quiet, but the problems faced will only metathesize.

Some diplomats may not even be cognizant of how their wishful thinking permeates analysis. The circles diplomats move in are exceedingly small: They meet other diplomats, business and cultural elites, and politicians. Few Western diplomats stationed in Ankara ever spend much time in Çinçin and the consuls in Istanbul avoid Sultanbeyli and Küçükçekmece. Even if they do symbolically visit such places once or twice in their posting, none of their contacts live there.

There is also a tendency among some diplomats to rationalize their lack of contacts and reach in that they must work with the ruling party, and too much outreach to broader society can antagonize their government contacts and make their missions more difficult. This was the context in which Ambassador Ross Wilson dismissed the Turkish opposition as a cacophony.

To counter such diplomatic distortions in assessing regressive regimes and authoritarian administrations, the best metric the United States and Western capitals can embrace is to assess how those countries treat their religious and ethnic minorities.

Religious freedom is often the canary in the coal mine that first confirms regimes' disdain for international norms. By this metric, Turkey is in a dire state. Yezidis, who have returned

FREEDOM CONVENTION

FREEDOM CONVENTION

to Iraq regularly, hear from middlemen and smugglers who can provide proof-of-life of kidnapped girls from their families. These girls now reside not only in regions of Syria controlled by Turkish proxies but also inside Turkey itself where they were sold to ideological sympathizers of the Islamic State who are protected by the Turkish government.

Whereas Turkish diplomats once spoke about the safety and security of Turkey's Jewish community, Turkish Jews are now emigrating and the community is dwindling. Simply put, it is logically inconsistent to cite a thriving Jewish community in order to affirm freedom and tolerance, but then fail to draw the opposite conclusion when the community declines precipitously.

The recent attacks on the Christian community are well-documented and extend far beyond the reconversion of the Hagia Sophia and the Chora Church into mosques, but also interference with Christian leadership,

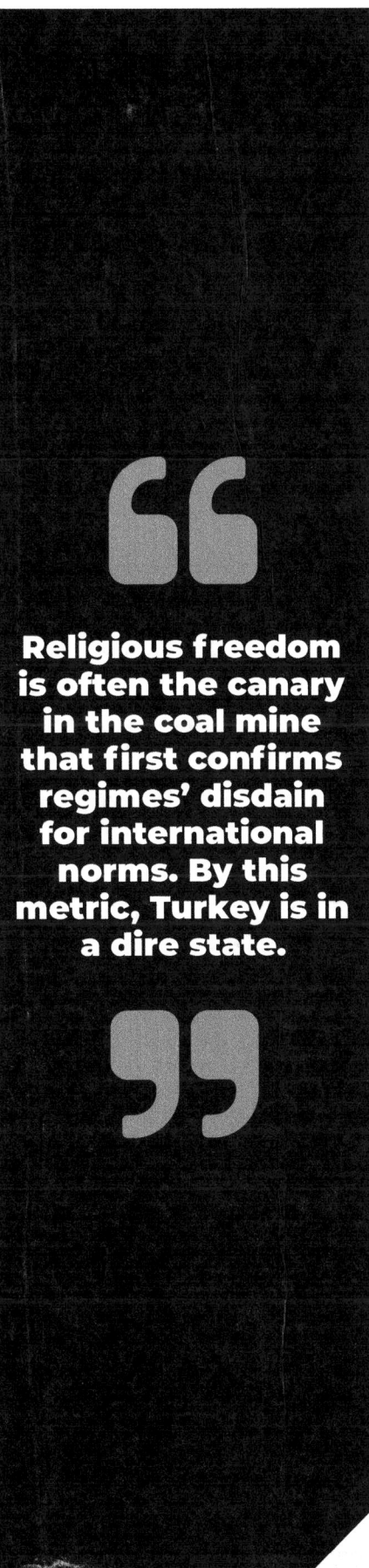

> **Religious freedom is often the canary in the coal mine that first confirms regimes' disdain for international norms. By this metric, Turkey is in a dire state.**

personnel, and finances.

The problem of religious freedom and minority rights is not limited to minority religions. The plight of the Alevi in Turkey remains underreported. Like the Ahmadi in Pakistan, the Turkish regime treats the Alevi worse than Christians and Jews because it refuses to recognize their theological status. Prayer halls are destroyed and children are forcibly indoctrinated during mandatory religious classes taught by Sunni instructors in grade schools. Erdoğan's repression of followers of exiled cleric Fethullah Gülen has far less to do with the supposed coup—that in many ways was a pretext constructed by Erdoğan and his followers to wage doctrinal warfare—than it does Erdoğan's Muslim Brotherhood-inspired vision which seeks to suppress the more traditional and moderate Anatolian Sufism which Gülen and his followers espouse. If Gülen's opponents want to counter the political vision which he espouses, the only effective way in the long-term is to wage a battle of ideas in a democratic debate rather than to slander and suppress.

On the ethnic basis, Erdoğan's followers increasingly target Kurds by suggesting that their more traditional, local practices make them enemies of Islam, hence Erdoğan blessing Turkish forces entering Syria to suppress Kurds as "the army of Muhammad" fighting those opposing Islam. Such tactics, which have ramifications inside Turkey itself, cynically twist religion by stigmatizing those who do not acquiesce to Erdoğan's political vision not simply as domestic political opponents, but rather as blasphemers who do not deserve the right to speak or even live.

Simply put, a quick survey of the state of religious and ethnic minorities inside Turkey suggests that Erdoğan's religious chauvinism has severely eroded the fabric of Turkish society and democracy. Given how Erdoğan's control of the media and education has indoctrinated the population (albeit not completely), Western diplomats would better serve both their home countries and Turkey by exploring how to repair the damage wrought by Erdoğan rather than waste any more time with debates about his intentions or whether Turkey is still a democratic republic.

FREEDOM CONVENTION

FREEDOM CONVENTION

CRAIG R. SHAGIN

Craig R. Shagin is an immigration lawyer in Harrisburg, Pennsylvania, and an Adjunct Professor of Law in Immigration Law and the Law of Asylum and Refugees at the Widener University Commonwealth Law School. He is an Honors graduate of Haverford College (1977) and Villanova University School of Law (1980). Mr. Shagin has authored numerous articles on immigration and nationality law and is on the Board of Editors of the AILA Law Journal.

I would like to begin by pointing out that I am involved in the private practice of law, immigration law, and asylum law in particular, and the message we've heard from Sümeyye Avcı (pg 37) corresponds with my own clients' statements and experiences. Turkey is a unique situation in this regard. Before July 15, 2016, I represented numerous Turkish clients, none of whom were particularly politically interested or involved. They were engineers, geologists, professors, businessmen, artists, and authors. People who, by and large, were in the U.S. with employment-based visas or were studying here. Near Harrisburg Pennsylvania, we have the U.S. Army War College, where several senior military officers in Turkey were also studying. I don't recall too many requests for asylum coming out of Turkey in the 20 years before July 15th, 2016. What I do recall is the occasional ethnic issue involving Kurds seeking asylum, but almost none of these cases involved politics and most of the clients I encountered would be highly sophisticated, well-educated, very productive members of Turkish society.

Then like a volcano or a sudden earthquake on July 15th, everything changed and it changed in extremely shocking ways. People who had dedicated their lives to the protection of Turkey in the military, very dedicated military officers at the war college, suddenly were ordered home, their family members arrested. It was quite clear that on July 16th that they had their names on the list to be subject to some kind of arrest or trial. Some of my clients, although by no means all, were involved in the Hizmet movement. Many were not military officers, these individuals had less knowledge about the situation than I did and were very apolitical. The only way you could describe their demeanor at the time of these events was one of shock and disbelief, that there must be an error, that they couldn't possibly think that they would be involved in a coup, that they would never do something like that, that they gave their lives to serving in a military that they truly believed in, and that they had absolutely zero interest in politics.

Worse, there was evidence that was coming forth very quickly of extreme measures taken against people without any regard for truth. How could a fourth-grade teacher possibly represent a threat to the government of Turkey? Why would you be arresting judges? What did a judge do that could possibly be a threat to Mr. Erdoğan or those ruling Turkey? What was the pattern here? Why would they be going after them? Of course, as a matter of presentation in court, we sort of had to know why they would be going after them, but we had difficulty understanding it because it was not something that our clients could make sense of as to why they would be considered a threat.

So that was an immediate response. As time went on, more and more clients had family members in Turkey. Some would escape through Iran and be in another country, gathering these families together. Even now we have clients who, for instance, have family members who were placed under arrest in an effort to get their husbands or other family members to return to Turkey, where they would then be arrested and presumably tortured. It's very shocking, it all happened very quickly. It is diabolical, the way this was thought-out. It was not something that happened slowly or by accident. Very often in cases of political persecution, it's a slow boil that goes up in temperature, but this one, as I said, was like a volcano. It happened immediately, it was well planned, it was well thought-out, and to this day, I don't think the world has responded in a uniform way that has been meaningful. >>>

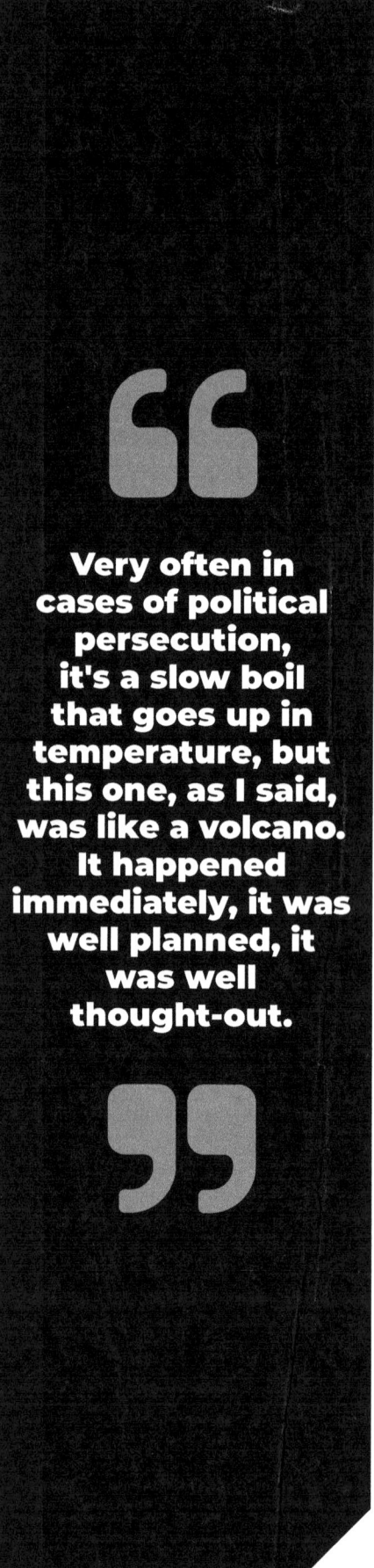

> **Very often in cases of political persecution, it's a slow boil that goes up in temperature, but this one, as I said, was like a volcano. It happened immediately, it was well planned, it was well thought-out.**

FREEDOM CONVENTION

FREEDOM CONVENTION

This brings me to my final point, which is the failure of the international refugee system to deal with the crisis that occurred out of Syria, that spread into Turkey, and now exists as a problem in Turkey itself. One of the powers that Turkey has in response to criticism is the threat of releasing another million or so people into Europe. This would not be a threat if the world had responded more effectively and affirmatively in dealing with the refugee crisis that came out of the Syrian Civil War.

We often say in class or as a theoretical proposition that one of the reasons for having an international system to deal with refugees, particularly war refugees, is to provide for greater political stability in the world. This is an excellent example of how that failure results in political instability. Similarly, the U.S. and other countries have really not been very helpful in reuniting these families in effective ways. This places the burden on other countries to deal with the refugees that are coming out of Turkey as a result of the political events that follow July 15th, 2016.

I think the main points that I would like to get across to people are that this was violent, fast, well thought-out, and resulted in widespread torture to the people who least deserved it. They had no relationship whatsoever at all with the supposed problems that were being used as an excuse to go after them. If the rest of the world remains silent, this problem is only going to continue to get worse. There is a way we can deal with it but it means we have to act cooperatively internationally and that seems to be very difficult for us now.

BÜLENT CEYHAN

Bülent Ceyhan has been a journalist in Turkey covering mostly criminal and social events in Turkey for nearly 20 years. He has reported about terrorist organizations, the mafia, government corruption, and deep state structuring. As of July 22, 2016, an arrest warrant was issued against him on charges of membership in a terrorist organization and faces at least 10 years in prison for his reporting on corruptions in the intelligence units and government of Turkey. He is now a refugee in Sweden. He currently writes reports on human rights violations.

The crime of torture in Turkey has aggravated significantly, especially after the coup attempt on 15 July 2016, and has become systematic again. The failure of the government to put forth an unwavering will to fight this crime has revealed a problem with impunity. Unfortunately, public officials who have been involved in torture for years are protected and rewarded with impunity by government agencies and officials. Even if they are prosecuted, they continue their official duties and even get promoted. They are prevented from being sentenced or going to prison for a range of varying excuses. Members of the judiciary and security forces believe that by covering up each others' crimes, they protect the so-called high interests of the state and prevent the state's name from being tarnished.

The increase in crimes of torture, which has been shown via reports of human rights organizations in Turkey in recent years, has now afflicted thousands of new victims. I have been preparing reports on torture victims for different human rights organizations for some time after my job as a journalist was ended by the lawsuits and arrest warrants brought against me. This work is psychologically taxing – each story I listen to puts a heavy burden on me. My concerns for how the victims of these abhorrent calamities will recover from their trauma are increasing.

One of the victims I interviewed was an academic. He was tortured for 7.5 months by MİT [the country's secret intelligence unit] in a secret place, where he was kidnapped and taken to. He was electrocuted, denied food and >>>

FREEDOM CONVENTION

FREEDOM CONVENTION

regular sleep, abused, and threatened with death. He told me that even his wife was not able to recognize him when he was released.

Another was kidnapped by the MİT and tortured in an unofficial interrogation center for 77 days. During the time he was deprived of his freedom, his family could not find out where he was. I do not want to describe the details of the torture, but there are those whose intestines were torn, those who could not use their limbs, and even died as a result of these actions. Teacher Gökhan Açıkkollu, for example, was subjected to severe torture in custody. His ribs were broken during interrogation, his medication was not given and he died in custody. Interestingly, less than hours after this murder committed in custody, the İstanbul Chief Public Prosecutor's Office declared that Açıkkollu died not because of torture, but because of health problems, without conducting any investigation and examining the evidence. But forensic reports documented torture.

Another striking story is the murder of a citizen named Murat Talk by torture by the accused police officer Oktay Kapsız, who worked as a commissioner in İstanbul Beşiktaş, and other police officers Ramazan Adıgüzel, Murat Ertürk, and Abdülcelil Karadağ. While on trial for the crime of torture, Oktay Kapsız was promoted as a 4th class security director. The case was settled in 2019 while he was serving as Chief of Police and he was sentenced to life in prison for murder by torture. He was not arrested. Oktay Kapsız continues to work in Muğla Police Department today and he, who killed a man with torture, was sent off to his place of duty with a state ceremony.

In addition to this, I spoke with police who quit the profession and witnessed the torture. A police officer, who did not want his name to be included in reports, explained that all of his superiors, including the Chief of Police, were aware of the tortures. According to what they said, torture instruments are also used in the interrogation rooms of the branches, in addition to giving electricity. Sometimes

> **This work is psychologically taxing – each story I listen to puts a heavy burden on me. My concerns for how the victims of these abhorrent calamities will recover from their trauma are increasing.**

people from MİT also participate in these interrogations to recruit people. The tortured persons are prevented from speaking during the health check. They are not left alone with the doctor, and even the doctors are threatened, preventing the traces of torture from entering the medical reports.

Another police officer described how the 33-year-old Limter-İş Union Education Specialist Süleyman Yeter was killed in custody on 7 March 1999. According to what he said, Yeter was killed by lying naked on a large ice slab taken from a fish market. According to what he said, some of the perpetrators did not even appear before a judge.

In a report we prepared for the AST recently to expose the torturers, we included the actions of some torturers, whose names have not been revealed until now, from court records. After the coup attempt on 15 July 2016, we deciphered the identities of people who tortured officers and non-commissioned officers. It is reported that the woman who tortured General Akın Öztürk intensely and whom even her colleagues had to stop her, yelling "it is enough", is Elif Sümercan, Deputy Chief of the TEM Branch. It turned out that the torturer Sümercan was later promoted and even appointed as the head of the department at the Ministry of Culture.

I continue to report people who are involved in the crime of torture in Turkey, who take action to protect the torturers, praise this crime and incite it. But as far as I can see, the government has made no effort to prevent this crime – on the contrary, they are making arrangements to facilitate it. I think that the words of AKP member Mehmet Metiner, Chairman of the Prison Subcommittee of the Turkish Parliament, when he said "we will not investigate the allegations of torture" in 2016, is an indicator of this attitude. I argue that international commissions should try more to prevent human rights violations in Turkey. I think a comprehensive struggle is needed so that the torturers sooner or later sit on the bench of the court and get the punishment they deserve. ∎

FREEDOM CONVENTION

FREEDOM CONVENTION

KERİM BALCI

Writer, journalist, academic, and human rights activist, Kerim Balcı is the Chief Advisor of London Based Human Rights Solidarity and works as a communication officer at London Advocacy, a litigation-based human rights advocacy firm. Balcı served as the editor in chief of Turkish Review, and as a columnist at Today's Zaman and Zaman dailies before these publications were shuttered by the Turkish government.

What happens when an oppressed minority comes into power without reconciliation taking place? I am going to discuss the AKP coming to power in Turkey without reconciliation, but this conversation is not only about Turkey, it's crucial for the future of Europe and the United States as well. We are likely going to see minorities become majorities within these countries within 20 to 40 years, and it is incredibly important that this happens peacefully.

Between 2002-2009 the traditional, so-called "Black Turks" of Turkey's socio-economic periphery moved to the center of the Turkish political system. They were not a distinct social group in the ethnic and linguistic sense but were grouped together and excluded from power. The secular elites regarded their religiosity as reminiscent of Ottoman backwardness. They evoked images of a Middle Eastern lifestyle, irrational beliefs, and oriental exoticisms. They were religious, they played oriental music, they did not use perfume, they left their shoes outside of their door stamps and scratched their stomachs in public. This was how the religious people in the rural areas were viewed by the secular elites. The secular elite on the other hand were the founders of the republic. They were the Westernizing, modernizing forces. They owned the land. They were urbanized, they were liberated from the shackles of Islam, and they were white. They listened to opera and watched ballet. Despite their status and perceived superiority, the white elites lost the mayoral elections in major cities in 1994. They then lost the general elections in 2002 and the Presidential Palace in 2007. They lost the army in 2008 and their last bastion of secularism, the Constitutional Court, was lost in 2010.

The black Turks were coming to power, but they were also becoming culturally white.

They developed an attitude of "revanchism", a term first used by Abdullah Gül, former president of Turkey. Unfortunately, while he warned against revanchism, he did nothing to stop it. The black Turks became white Turks, internalizing almost all of the discriminatory policies of the previous allies of authoritarianism. The old elite, for example, would accuse the old minority of becoming the long arm of Iranian and Saudi regimes. The new elite in turn now accuses the secular opposition of being the proxies of Western imperialism. The old elite labeled the so-called Black Turks backward, anti-modernization, and anti-democracy. The new elite accuse the old elite of conspiring against the rise of the "New Turkey", against a third airport in Istanbul, against the Channel Istanbul Project, against every attempt of technological revolution this "New Turkey" is attempting. Meanwhile the old elite forge or at least exaggerate stories about "a secret agenda" of the old minority.

A major problem with revanchism is that when power is transferred, retaliation is always expected, thus any degree of shifting power becomes an unacceptable loss. In 2015, the AKP government did not accept the results of the general election where it merely lost the parliamentary majority, as a result, they pushed for a re-run. In March 2019, they didn't accept the results of the İstanbul mayoral election and pushed for another re-run. This time the strategy backfired and they lost by an even larger margin. Undeterred, Erdoğan continues to manipulate the political field to guarantee that the mayors of opposition parties are not able to rule. There are vital lessons for the whole world that can be gleaned from our experience of shifting power.

Let me move to another issue that pertains to the tensions that rise out of different minority groups >>>

> **The black Turks became white Turks, internalizing almost all of the discriminatory policies of the previous allies of authoritarianism. The old elite, for example, would accuse the old minority of becoming the long arm of Iranian and Saudi regimes. The new elite in turn now accuses the secular opposition of being the proxies of Western imperialism.**

FREEDOM CONVENTION

campaigning for differing degrees of rights and autonomy. I am going to use some terminology from 1949-1950 from the UN Human Rights Commission Memorandum. Category A is defined as "a minority group that asks only for non-discrimination". They just want to be equal citizens under the law. Largely, the Jewish and the Christian minorities of Turkey are Category A minorities. They don't ask for any special treatment, they don't want autonomy, they just want to be equal citizens. When it comes to the Kurds, a majority of the Kurdish population in Turkey is now in Category B, they want some special rights, they want to use their mother-tongue in education. Some of them want certain levels of political, socio-economic, or at least cultural autonomy. There is also Category C, which the United Nations doesn't accept. Category C minorities are separationist movements. PKK was at one point a Category C Kurdish minority. There are Kurds who fit into all of the categories above and also experience constant shifts between these categories in the eyes of the Justice and Development Party. When the Justice and Development Party came to power, PKK had already declared a unilateral cease-fire, and it was moving away from Category C into Category B. They were at the mild end of Category B. They were only looking for linguistic and cultural rights and a kind of trust-building process where they were able to speak about regional and local governance, they were not speaking about autonomy at all.

There were difficult times between 2005 and 2009. In 2009, the AKP regime launched the so-called "solution process" and it was a light at the end of the tunnel. They called it, "The Kurdish Opening". This involved large-scale public consultations, and for committees of wise men to be established. Kurdish names of villages were reinstituted, even the city of Tunceli was once again called "Dersim". In 2009, Gül referred to Iraqi Kurdistan with its proper name for the first time. For some time it had been referred to only as "the structure in Northern Iraq" and once again this is its official referent. Even PM Erdoğan at that time said "if my ancestors, the Ottomans, didn't have a problem with the term Kurdistan, why should I have a problem?". A week before the time of writing, president Erdoğan said, "there is no Kurdish problem in Turkey". This means there are no Kurds in Turkey because there are problems as long as no one acknowledges the Kurds. Instead of acknowledging that there is a particular minority group being oppressed, the AKP says things like "we might have some rule of law problems, we might have some problems in our democracy, but we are going to pass through a reform process". That's what the current government is promising but has made clear that it is not going to do. The whole process is a complete denial of the existence of the Kurdish minority.

By and large, the AKP regime completely canceled the recognition and reconciliation process in 2015. Why? Because they lost the election. Well, to be clear, they won elections, but they lost the parliamentary majority and persecuted the Kurds for voting against them. This did not just happen with the Kurds. There was an attempt at reconciliation with the Alawite people between 2008 and 2015, the Alevi population of Turkey was extremely hopeful alongside the Greek Orthodox and Syrian Orthodox populations of Turkey as they understood that by reconciling with the minorities, the Turkish government was moving away from the traditional exclusionary policies. Unfortunately after 2015, when the AKP government lost the majority of the parliament, they began to ignore, persecute, and turn their backs on minorities because they failed to have a single party government. They betrayed the process and they adopted a new strategy of strong-arming Category B Kurds into becoming Category A Kurds. Meaning they needed to establish their own party, an Islamist Kurdish party that was not looking for Kurdish language privileges, that did not push for cultural or political rights but just for citizenship rights. Those who did not join Category A push for citizenships alone - meaning the majority of legitimate Kurdish politicians - were pushed towards Category C. The former leader of HDP, in fact all the members of the HDP, are behind the bars nowadays and they are being treated as terrorists - meaning Category C. Whenever the Turkish president speaks about HDP politicians, he categorically denies them being either Category A or B minorities but labels them Category C minority.

I have a few words to say about another minority that is likely to be the source of a huge headache in Turkey's future, that is Syrian Arabs. Up until very recently when speaking about minorities in Turkey the Alawite people would be the most likely to come up, after the Kurds, due to discrimination against the Alawite population in Sunni religious education. The Syrian Arabs in Turkey are largely Sunni Arabs and it would seem that the Turkish government wouldn't have any problem with integrating them into the overall system. At the moment they are not asking for any special treatment; they are a Category-A minority. They want employment, health insurance, and so on. The government's response is to give them these rights. I also have to say Turkey did a fantastic job by accepting more than three million Syrian Arabs into Turkey. But keeping this minority integrated with the overall society is a tough task, and if you start to use some of the Syrian Arabs as mercenaries in Libya and more recently in Armenia and Azerbaijan, you begin pushing them towards becoming Category C. It seems incredibly likely that the Syrian Arabs are not going to move to Category B, they are going to jump over Category B and many of them will become eventually mobs, gangs, and terrorists in the long run, because are they used by the Turkish government as militants.

Another sign of trouble when it comes to Syrian Arabs and Turkey is the fact we have a history with Syrian Arabs in Turkey, they have belonged to the Alawites. These individuals are different from the Turkish Alawites, they are Arabic Alawites, which are by and large aShia sect, and they are fighting with each other. With the kind of government we have in Turkey, President Erdoğan moving towards an ultra-nationalist ideology, the patron of the government being MHP - an ultra-nationalist party, the government is looking for groups to label as terrorists within Turkey. This is because the current government does not recognize minority Category B as legitimate categories, and they push them either towards becoming Category C separatist movements or becoming de-politicized entities with no particular minority identities. It seems to me that the future of Turkey is a gloomy affair.

FREEDOM CONVENTION

FREEDOM CONVENTION

MEHMET EFE ÇAMAN

Dr. Mehmet Efe Çaman studied at Ludwig-Maximilians-Universitaet Muenchen (LMU) and Augsburg University, where he earned his combined B.A./M.A. degree. In 2005 he obtained his Ph.D. as a "Bavarian State Elite Research Doctoral Scholar" at Augsburg University. His current research focuses on authoritarianism, democratization, and human rights as well as on Turkish politics in comparative politics and international political contexts.

I will be talking about the Kurdish problem and I will particularly focus on domestic and international dimensions. My main focus is going to be Turkey's Kurdish policies, particularly in Syria. I will be discussing and talking about racist and ethnic Turkish nationalism a little bit, then I will move towards the Kurds in Syria and Ankara's position. And I will be addressing domestic policymakers, the regime, the Kurdish problem, and also some human rights dimensions. Then, I will finalize some projections for the future.

I'd like to focus on the current Kurdish domestic and foreign policy dimensions of Turkey. To better understand Turkey's Syria policy towards Syrian Kurds, the relation to domestic politics, and the Turkey regime we must look at historic events and the changes in Ankara's Kurdish policy. Let's focus on the prehistory of Turkey; the Ottoman Empire.

Since the beginning, with the Ottoman Empire's nationalist policies in the early 20th century, constructing a unified and homogenous Turkish state has been a priority of the Turkish government. The Ottoman Empire lost its territories almost entirely due to the irredentist policies of Enver, Talat, and Cemal pashas during the war. Eventually, the empire collapsed. This legacy of Turkish nationalists was inherited by the new Republic, founded by Mustafa Kemal Atatürk who made Turkish nationalism one of the six principles of its ideology, which is called "Kemalism". This ideological principle considers the Turkish nation the only entity of the Republic, unifying a monolithic and homogenized people, that was the goal.

Accordingly, all other ethnic identities other than Turkish were rejected. Advocating for minority rights was criminalized. In political practice, both the

Armenian Genocide of 1915 and the deportation of Greeks according to the Population Exchange Convention of 1923 contributed to the design of a more homogenous Turkey. To create a homogenous society, this mindset utilized both ethnic cleansing and assimilation policies. It is very typical in the 20th Century. Advocating minority rights of other nationalities was criminalized. Kemalist Turkish nationalism was a contribution to late Ottoman social engineering. That aimed to diminish all ethnic identities other than Turkish.

The primary domestic security concerns of the Turkish state have been, accordingly, 1) preventing non-Turkish ethnic groups from influencing policies and politics and the public sphere; 2) denying any kind of cultural minority rights. Based on these nationalist policies, the existence of Kurds, Arabs, and other ethnic groups was denied and their language, culture, folklore, music, art, literature, and history were prohibited in the public sphere. Turkish nationalism has been very influential not only in domestic politics but also in the foreign and security policy of Turkey, particularly, after the beginning of the armed insurgency of the Kurdish Workers Party (PKK) in the 1980s. That declared the goal of a separate state of Kurds.

Turkey's security agenda during the 1980s and 1990s identified Kurdish separatism as "the most dangerous major threat to the country". This led to more radical and sophisticated securitization of the Kurdish issue. It also strengthened the position of the military and civilian bureaucracy in political decision-making processes in all security policy-related policy fields. A core element of this military-civilian bureaucracy, called "the deep state", obtained excessive power and controlled almost all security-related policy areas. The deep states used the instruments of the dictate regime designed by the Turkish Constitution of 1982, such as the National Security Council in other ways. Their goal was to subordinate civilians in security-related policy areas, particularly in >>>

> **Most of the Turkish government and society accepted the deep state role as well as its hawkish position on the Kurdish issue: a position that accepted only a military solution.**

FREEDOM CONVENTION

domestic and foreign Kurdish policy-related topics.

Most of the Turkish government and society accepted the deep state role as well as its hawkish position on the Kurdish issue: a position that accepted only a military solution. In the 1990s, Turkish foreign policymakers held Syria responsible for giving external support to Kurdish separatists, to the PKK. Apart from sheltering Abdullah Öcalan, the leader of PKK, Syria also allowed PKK militants to use Syrian territory for their training camps, from where the PKK entered Turkish territory to commit attacks. Back then, approximately a third of PKK militants were of Syrian origin. For Turkey's military solution strategy, terminating the existence of the PKK in Syria was essential. PKK leadership, particularly Öcalan, lived between 1984 and 1999 in Syria, and in 1999 Turkey increased its pressure on the Syrian government to extradite him, threatening military action. Öcalan was expelled by Damascus under this enormous pressure from Ankara and he was captured in Nairobi, Kenya, and was brought to Turkey.

Turkey-Syria relations improved particularly after the AKP came to power in 2002. The AKP prioritized a regionally oriented foreign policy that focused on Turkey's historical and cultural roots with its close neighbors. There was a remarkable moderation and remarkable new policies in Turkish foreign policies towards Syria until the Arab Spring destabilized the country, Syria, in 2012. During the first ten years of the AKP era, Turkey experienced significant democratization and de-secularization that created a new perception of constructive and cooperation-oriented foreign policy that paved the way for diminishing the range of enemies and gaining more life in Turkey. At the same time, Turkey initiated the normalization of civil-military relations in the framework of Turkey's EU process, which required the military to be subordinate to elected political decision-makers. This way, the deep state gradually lost its influence and for many years Ankara externalized the problems of Kurdish separatism onto Syria. The AKP government changed this and opened the door for more cooperation and, among other things, this progress was the result of the EU process and the associated democratization. A systematic transformation and a proportion of EU norms and principles in the regional policies.

It was during the AKP rule that Ankara and Damascus elevated a visa requirement within the framework of the high-level strategic cooperation in 2009. Relations reached such a major level, even joint cabinet meetings were organized between the two countries. For the first time in its history, Turkey had adopted a discourse and an economic integration with a neighboring country. But these ambitious policies were challenged by the Arab Spring. Up until the Arab Spring, the AKP had overlooked the undemocratic nature of the Damascus regime. When the mass protests spread to Syria, Ankara first tried to convince the Assad regime to carry out reforms to a democratized, open political system and was hopeful that its advice would be taken into account. But when Assad insisted on remaining its regime, AKP started to take a tougher line and ended up backing Sunni Islamist rebels, fighting to overthrow the Assad regime. Particularly, after Erdoğan increased its power in Turkey and de-facto started to govern the country with his presidential decrees, Ankara intensified its support drastically.

WOMEN'S RIGHTS IN TURKEY

FREEDOM CONVENTION

FREEDOM CONVENTION

EREN KESKİN, Esq.

Atty. Eren Keskin has been a lawyer since 1984 and has been actively involved in human rights defense since 1989. She served as Istanbul Branch President and Vice President of the Human Rights Association, IHD, and currently serves as İHD Co-Chairwoman. Keskin is also the founder of an office that advocates for women and transgender women free of charge since 1997.

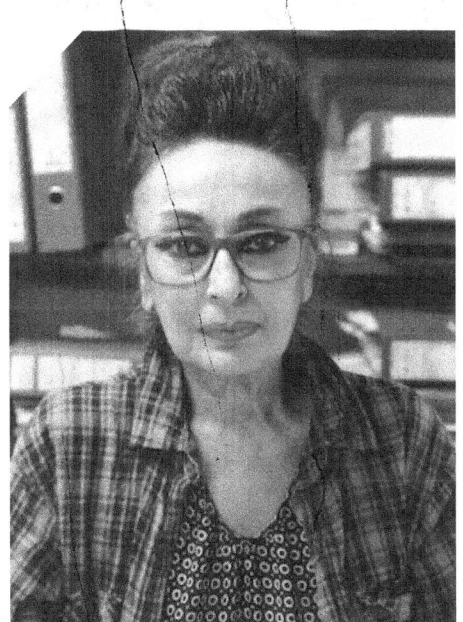

The first and greatest atrocity of the century was committed in Turkey; the 1915 Armenian Genocide. Followed by the 1938 Dersim Genocide. We live in a climate heavy with the stench of death and genocide. In all these horrific genocide events, the most victimized sufferers were women. This land is full of women's graves. I wanted this point, above all, to be very clear.

Unfortunately, our legal system is organized according to the Turkish and Sunni Muslim identity; a feudal and militaristic official ideology that is extremely masculine. This written legal system is one in which women are generally ignored. Until 2005, the Turkish Penal Code had little regulation of violence against Turkish women, no definition of sexual harassment, a grossly inadequate definition of rape, and murdering a woman out of honor could actually reduce a sentence. Violence against women was solely regulated within the framework of general morality and family crimes.

In 2005, huge improvements were made to the Turkish Penal Code due to the struggles of women as well as the rapprochement with the European Union. For the first time, sexual assault and sexual harassment were both defined and labeled criminal. And murdering a woman for honor was no longer rewarded. Then, in 2011 the Turkish Republic signed the İstanbul Convention of the European Council Preventing and Combating Violence against Women and Domestic Violence. The greatest impact of the İstanbul Convention was the provision that customs, traditions, and a sense of honor cannot be considered a reason for violence against women. Turkey signed it. Unfortunately, the Republic of Turkey is not a state of law. That is, it does not apply international conventions, which have binding power over even its own written law and Constitution. Turkey signs them but does not implement them in practice. This is our biggest problem [Turkey withdrew from the contract with the Presidential Decision No. 3718 published in the Official Gazette on March 20, 2021 on the grounds that the convention was in conflict with the country's social and moral norms and traditions].

I founded a law firm in 1997 that provides free legal representation to women who have been sexually tortured by state forces such as police, soldiers, and village guards. To date, 758 women and transgender women have appealed to us. This number only scratches the surface because women are often ashamed, afraid, and do not disclose the sexual violence or torture they experience. Many are terrified because if the perpetrator is one of the state forces they are offered great impunity. We have been working since 1997, so far, apart from the 2 village guards, not one state official has been sentenced. It is an official ideology that is so decisive and dominating that it makes all people believe in it.

Currently, the state of the Republic of Turkey does not comply with any international convention it signs, including its own domestic law. For example, if the İstanbul Convention, was actually applied and enforced, much could be done in terms of violence against women. But the Republic of Turkey refused to implement this convention. Judges and prosecutors act as if this contract does not exist and unfortunately Turkey is not adequately supervised in this sense so nothing is being done.

We say that violence against women is political. Why is it political? The state has a very masculine, harsh style. Turkey's Interior Minister Süleyman Soylu recently made the following statement: "I gave the order [to the police] to cut him to pieces when you catch him." This clearly means "I instructed them to torture". An increase in violence against >>>

> **Our prisons are filled with women today. There are left-wing women, Kurdish women, and women alleged to be members of the Gülen movement.**

FREEDOM CONVENTION

FREEDOM CONVENTION

women can be expected in a regime that would take this kind of action against someone. Our prisons are filled with women today. There are left-wing women, Kurdish women, and women alleged to be members of the Gülen movement. Many are sick women whose illnesses cannot be documented with the reports of Forensic Medicine, an official expert institution. They have been imprisoned and their human rights usurped.

Today is the day of human rights. We are holding this meeting on the day when a universal declaration is accepted. But none of the articles here will be applied in Turkey. At this point, I would like to touch on international control mechanisms. The İstanbul Convention, which is the most advanced convention in the field of violence against women, and the control mechanism of this convention, Grevio's report on Turkey has been published. The Council of Europe remains silent on this negative report, and I criticize it. Unfortunately, interests determine the relations between states and there is an extremely male-dominated system all over the world. That's why women need solidarity at the international level so much. All of us have a great responsibility to realize this solidarity.

HİLAL AKDENİZ

Hilal Akdeniz is a sociologist and lives in Germany. Her Grandfather came as a migrant guest-worker to Germany in the early 1970s. She studied sociology in Germany and Switzerland on topics including flight, migration, identity, and gender. She works at the Foundation for Dialogue and Education in Berlin. For her Ph.D., she is currently researching human rights violations during arrests and prison sentences after the coup of July 15, 2016 in Turkey.

Women are arrested every day in Turkey. Women are arrested just for helping victims, women are taken from the delivery room by the police and taken to a prison.

There are approximately 246,000 people in prison in Turkey, of whom about 4 percent are women. That is approximately 12,000 women in prison. This number has increased several times compared to previous years. As a sociologist, I couldn't just watch all this from the sidelines. Last year, I made a call live on Twitter to document the human rights violations and torture occurring in Turkey as best I could. For my Ph.D. I conducted nearly 40 biographically narrated interviews with those who were detained after the 2016 failed coup attempt or who had served a prison sentence on charges of terrorism. A surprising number of interviewees from Turkey contacted me. They said they could not stand the indifference of the media and the legal system towards them and they asked me to tell their story and share their pain. I would like to thank all my interview partners for their trust.

I would like to present the reality of what happens to these detained women and children, the forms of violence and torture they have been subjected to in prison. I want to talk about social sanctions and discrimination and those who are affected by them. I will also give a brief summary of the results I have achieved so far.

After the failed coup attempt in July 2016, Turkey declared a State of Emergency, which lasted for almost two years, during which time Turkey's law and democracy were dismantled. The period of pre-trial detention was >>>

FREEDOM CONVENTION

FREEDOM CONVENTION

increased to 30 days. This means that people are subjected to harassment, torture, and beatings for 30 days without being able to see their families and lawyers. Sometimes it means they detain 40 people in 15-square-meter wards with no windows, adequate beds, or space for other necessities. Prisoners only get water twice a day and do not have access to enough food. They cannot shower. There are not enough facilities for toilets. Under these conditions, 30 days is like an eternity. The people I interviewed told me that they were threatened with rape and violence and badly abused every day. They said that during the initial admission everyone was subjected to a detailed nude search. The interviewees also spoke of sexual harassment and verbal attacks during the interrogations.

The AKP government frequently raises the issue of hijab and wants to position itself as the protector of the hijab in the country. But all the people I interviewed spoke through tears of being forced to remove their headscarves despite the presence of male civil servants. Some women still had small babies that were not weaned, and when detained, they had to leave their babies with family members because they thought they would be back again in a few hours. Some of these women were not allowed to breastfeed their babies, so they had to spill their milk in the sinks of police stations or prisons. They did not receive the necessary medical care when they had a high fever and breast infections. Women with babies or accompanying children were not given proper food. Unfortunately, these unfavorable conditions for children continue in prisons.

Many children under the age of six are in prison with their mothers. They are deprived of amenities such as toys, meals, and activities for toddlers. Toys are prohibited in the wards. For this reason, some women make toys for their children from plastic bottles or similar materials. Frequently the handmade objects made by political prisoners and even the flowers they

> **The people I interviewed told me that they were threatened with rape and violence and badly abused every day. They said that during the initial admission everyone was subjected to a detailed nude search. The interviewees also spoke of sexual harassment and verbal attacks during the interrogations.**

plant are taken away by the guards; any beautification in the cells is confiscated by the guards. Many mothers told me that they were completely overwhelmed by their situation. They are often depressed. They say that they cannot show the necessary attention and care to their children and that they cannot adequately respond to their needs. In some cases, other imprisoned women look after their children for a few hours, showing their solidarity and support.

I would like to mention two specific examples from my research. A young mother told me that her first night in prison with her son was the longest night of her life. The guards did not give her the necessary supplies that she had bought for her son; they said they should check everything first. She was sent to prison that morning, and in the evening she asked the guards again if they had finished checking her bag. She said the baby's pacifier and bottle were in the bag and the baby couldn't sleep without them. The guard shouted at him. The baby cried for hours and the mother could not do anything for the baby. She said she lost her belief that there is good in people that night.

The second example is about another mother. She was trying not to make her child feel scared or overwhelmed during their stay in prison with her four-year-old son. She was telling him that she was there to work and that they would go home as soon as she was done. Her son was asking her why she had to work so long every day and when they would go home. When they were finally released and went home, the boy asked his mother if they had enough money. The mother was taken aback and asked her son why he was asking this question. The son was afraid that if his mother did not have enough money, she would have to return to work.

This difficult situation in Turkish prisons has become even more strenuous during the COVID-19 pandemic. Medical care is neglected, and open contact visits are almost completely forbidden, except for a few phone calls where these women can talk to their families. Few in Turkish society nor the world are aware of these tragedies. It is easy enough to believe that these people have suffered very little damage and that they will return to their normal lives when they are released. Unfortunately, this is not the case. All of these individuals were caught as terrorist suspects and labeled as terrorists in the state archives. When they apply to open a bank account or a job, the system displays their criminal record as a "terrorist". Therefore, they cannot live independent, free, and self-determined lives in Turkey. Worse still, they won't be able to live in Turkey and they can't apply for passports as they are banned from traveling due to their criminal record.

Unfortunately, these people are not warmly received by their social circles when they are released. Some people are not afraid to hurl hate speech or insults, while many others are afraid of meeting or contacting them. They fear that if they help the accused, they will be accused, punished, and even become "terrorists" like them. For example, when people visit those in prison, even when they donate food, they are publicly punished and branded as terrorists by the media. Many interviewees shared the >>>

FREEDOM CONVENTION

FREEDOM CONVENTION

emotional difficulties they experienced due to discrimination both from and towards their families or friends.

These women, who are often well-educated and highly qualified, generally do not have a choice but to do jobs such as cleaning and preparing meals for very low wages. They are often shamefully discriminated against by their employers, who hired them as informal workers without any insurance or job security. Women who are accused of being terrorists or whose husbands are in prison encounter a lot of hardships; they also face the threat of sexual abuse as well as financial difficulties. Therefore, it is not surprising that some of the interviewees mentioned social genocide when describing their situation. Almost none of them can imagine a future in Turkey. Only three of the interviewees wanted to continue living in Turkey. They believe that the rule of law and legal justice has been completely destroyed.

When the police called on these women for questioning, they thought there was a mistake, that they would return home in a few hours. None of them had ever experienced police brutality, torture, or prison. Some of them have suffered psychological damage from harassment and torture in prison that will affect them throughout their lives. All of the people I interviewed experienced marginalization either from their friends or family. This has done profound emotional damage to many of them. None of the interviewees talked about feelings and thoughts such as violence and revenge while sharing their experiences and adopted non-violent methods in expressing their protests. Individuals admitted that they had lacked solidarity with minorities or an understanding of democracy before being imprisoned. They said they would be more active in contributing to such values in the future. ■

VONYA WOMACK

Vonya Womack is Executive Director of (RUSU) Refugees Unknown-Stories Untold and a Human Rights Activist. She is an international presenter and keynote speaker and a committed advocate for women and children and those who have experienced trauma as refugees. She is a published author in academic research journals, with a recent book chapter "Trauma of Turkish Women and Children in an Era of Political Unrest" in a new book titled Human Rights in Turkey, Assaults on Human Dignity.

Turkey has had their parliamentary system replaced with a new system that is ever increasingly controlled by President Recep Tayyip Erdoğan. Erdoğan's authoritarian shift over the last several years has seen Turkish citizens silenced and its media outlets and journalists demonized. He has gone as far as restricting or blocking social media sites and kidnapping Hizmet supporters overseas. His threats know no boundaries, and his rhetoric has demonized this group of citizens. For those of you who may be reading that are not familiar with this movement called Hizmet, which means Service, I can best describe it to you as a global movement that focuses on science education, volunteerism, community involvement, social work, and interfaith and intercultural dialogue. I am honored to know some of them.

For Hizmet supporters prior to and definitely after the coup in 2016, they have had to live daily with the fear of losing their jobs and having no means of income, fear of threats of arrest, fear of torture in prison, and fear of other family members or friends becoming targets. It is perception that matters most for Erdoğan. Put his political opponents in jail, create a community of hate towards others, and ultimately maintain authoritarian power. Most of all, and what I want to touch on in this presentation, is the severity of the unraveling of the Turkish laws, especially when it comes to human rights where women and children are involved.

One of the many areas where the laws in place are completely ignored surrounds Turkish prisons. There are countless reports from those who have been in prison or who are currently in prison, >>>

FREEDOM CONVENTION

FREEDOM CONVENTION

even from some of the world's best known human rights organizations that no law is upheld within Turkey's prisons and that those who work within them will do as they see fit with their prisoners. The human rights abuses coming out of these prisons are increasing and we must call attention to them on a broader global scale.

When speaking to women who have been in these prisons, one hears stories of tiny holding cells with people packed in, often without enough room to even sleep on the floor. With deteriorating prison structures and overcrowded prison cells, the air smelled of stale cement, dirt, mold, and sometimes feces. Perhaps this is because those who came into the prison had to walk through the sewer that seeped outside the buildings, or maybe it was the elderly woman sitting in a plastic chair in the corner who was not allowed to have her wheelchair with a puddle of urine and feces pooled at her feet. Messes like this are common and not having been cleaned endangers everyone in the cell. As I sat and listened to the most personal stories of prison experiences by these most noble, strong, and courageous women, I became drawn to this very dark and emotionally destructive place. A place of losing one's sense of purpose.

I know those stories are very hard to hear for many of you reading today, and for others this may be one of the first times you have heard about the Hizmet Movement and how these highly educated, giving, and kind people are being persecuted.

Over the past 6-7 years there has been an increase of incredible human rights violations documented and endured by women in prisons. There are more than 17,000 women and nearly 400 children under the age of 6 in prisons today. This is due to trumped-up charges that they were part of a larger plot to overthrow the regime. Erdoğan has used the Hizmet Movement as a scapegoat to devise his coup attempt to maintain his political power.

Erdoğan has not condemned human rights violations against women and children in these prisons. In fact, in

> **First, we can be a voice for those who can't use theirs. We can lift those voices before human rights organizations and government officials and continuously remind them of the human rights violations in Turkey.**

April, he allowed the release of tens of thousands of prisoners with charges as horrifying as murder and assault to ease overcrowding and to protect detainees and workers from COVID-19. The bill that was passed excluded those imprisoned on terrorism charges, which is what Erdoğan's accusation towards Hizmet supporters. So, the mothers and children have had to stay in prison during the COVID-19 crisis. Even pregnant women, those who have just given birth, and those who have serious medical problems were not exempt. It is a way for Erdoğan to get to the men in the Hizmet movement. Therefore, he has encouraged multifarious human rights violations, including sexual assault of women, beatings of children, and deteriorating, overcrowded prison cells. Let me be clear that I am saying that Erdoğan is encouraging human rights violations, not preventing them.

To keep his power and continue with his autocratic government he has placed the lives of some of the most educated Turkish citizens in grave danger. He continues to have people hunted like animals. I have heard stories from those who have experienced being sought out at the schools where they teach, the universities where they were administrators, courtrooms where they were judges and lawyers, offices where they were doctors and surgeons, businesses where they were executives or workers, and government offices where they held prominent political positions representing their communities or their country. For those who have been affected by the illegal crackdown, it is the knowledge of prison conditions and the facts of torture that eventually push them to flee the country leaving all they have and know to seek a life of freedom.

There are some things that I believe we can do to help build a stronger vocal democracy on a global platform and help to create better and more reliable safeguards for universal human rights. First, we can be a voice for those who can't use theirs. We can lift those voices before human rights organizations and government officials and continuously remind them of the human rights violations in Turkey. We can put pressure on organizations like the United Nations and call out countries like Turkey that abuse the very systems they have agreed to protect. If global agencies would hold those who perpetrate human rights violations accountable, then it would become a gold standard to uphold those rights. Along with this accountability comes a trickle-down effect into societies so that there can then be more acceptance of different ideologies, different cultures, and customs. This can create a world of tolerance for differences among us and ultimately lead to peace and treating others with human dignity. ∎

FREEDOM CONVENTION

FREEDOM CONVENTION

ARLET NATALİ AVAZYAN

Natali Avazyan describes herself as a believer, a Christian who tries to shape her life in the way of Jesus Christ and her teachings. A Turkish citizen of Armenian origin, Avazyan is a human rights champion, an activist, who dedicated her life to fighting for the rights of women and children in particular, without revealing their identities.

I am going to speak as a person who had witnessed first-hand the genocide towards women and children in this country over the last five years.

I want to begin with a quote from the Holy Book. The Holy Book says: "Woman had been created from the rib bone of Adam". It doesn't say leg or any other part of the body, it says the rib because it holds our life. Also, Prophet Muhammed (PBUH) said that "Heavens are under the feet of the mothers". This is how the holy book talks about women. Unfortunately, in Turkey, it is the opposite. Women wake up in the morning and find themselves accused of terrorism or they will be accused of making propaganda for a terrorist organization. Many are eventually detained. These women are often accused of being leftist or members of the Gülen movement.

Let me give you a very small example. I wrote on social media about a proposition by the journalist Hilal Kaplan, well-known for her close relationship with the government. Just because I talked about a suggestion by Kaplan, my mother's house was raided by a police team, which I counted to have at least 18 police officers. I was in Adana that day for Ahmet Burhan Ataç [Ataç was a cancer patient boy whose father was in prison and whose mother was not allowed to accompany him for treatment abroad. He died longing for his father.] and I returned to find that my house had been raided.

You are detained, they strip you naked in a very humiliating way, you are examined with 3 sit and stand commands. I was subjected to this treatment just because I said a word to Hilal Kaplan. I will leave what is done to the female members of the Gülen movement to your imagination. Unfortunately, there have been tens of thousands of women who have been treated the same way or even worse. As we know there have been at least 780 babies in prison with their mothers.

What I cannot comprehend is why are the European Union, United States, and United Nations all silent and are not doing anything about it. They are not even talking about it when mothers in our country are put in prisons with their kids. These women are isolated and left alone, especially the ones who are followers of the Gülen movement.

As I am talking here, there is a reality that the police may come and arrest me, take me away. This might very well happen just because I am supporting these women. Unfortunately, no women's rights organizations come in support of these women. As a leftist and Christian, I am trying to help them. In the last five years, a lot of things have been left unfinished, all the dreams incomplete, parents couldn't be with their children, and children's dreams are incomplete. Many know our struggle regarding Ahmet Burhan Ataç, we had everything in our hands but we could not help him live. We struggled so much, we fought to send him abroad for treatment. We were not able to get a passport for his mother. If they allowed us, which they didn't, maybe this child would be alive today.

When the boat of Feridun Maden sank and he was drowned along with the families on board, a lifeless body hit the shore. Feridun was wearing blue socks. Ever since that day, I cannot buy blue socks for any kid.

Dreams have been strangled. In one conversation, Ahmet was asking his mother, "Will I recover from cancer?" His mother said, "Yes you will for sure." Ahmet asked another question: "How many months do we have left until the summer?" The answer was, "We have two months left". Ahmet asked again, "Mom, could I ride my cycle this summer?" His mother responded, "Yes, you will". But this conversation was one month before Ahmet's death. Ahmet did not recover, he did not see the summer and unfortunately, he did not ride his bicycle. >>>

> **What I cannot comprehend is why are the European Union, United States, and United Nations all silent and are not doing anything about it. They are not even talking about it when mothers in our country are put in prisons with their kids.**

FREEDOM CONVENTION

FREEDOM CONVENTION

I have tried to help Fatih Terzioglu and we lost him in August 2020. I know his case quite well. The only accusation against him was donating money after the earthquake in Van. I also know Esra as well, his wife, she is a young woman and they have two kids. Their father, Fatih, was in prison. After months Fatih was released because he had cancer; Fatih and Esra had a chance to see each other and Fatih said, "There is a TV series I want you to watch at home and I will watch it at the hospital so that we can feel like we are together like a family." They never came together because he died.

Selman was another small victim, who also died from cancer, a brain tumor. His father was in prison and his crime was teaching literature. Yes, he was persecuted for being a teacher. He worked in a university prep course as a teacher. I struggled, worked so hard so that Selman could see his father. His only wish was to see his father. Finally, I was able to successfully advocate for this time and his father came to the house where Selman was, along with an armed escort. But by this point, it was too late. Selman had already lost consciousness.

There are so many stories that I would like to tell, but ultimately I simply want the United Nations to do what they are supposed to do to these children. Unfortunately, there is a terrible claim that they do not have children in prison, so mothers have to share their food with their kids. I do not want to go to children's funerals anymore, I want to celebrate their birthdays.

SOPHIA PANDYA

Sophia Pandya is a professor and department chair at California State University at Long Beach, in the Department of Religious Studies. Winner of the 2016 Advancement of Women Award at CSULB from the President's Commission on the Status of Women, she received her BA from UC Berkeley in Near Eastern Studies/Arabic, and her MA and Ph.D. from UC Santa Barbara in Religious Studies. A Fulbright Scholar, she specializes in women and Islam, and more broadly in contemporary movements within Islam.

Dr. Angela Raven-Roberts asserts that during a political conflict, women in particular suffer from displacement, poverty, and sexual abuse. They are also used as tools to create fear and dishonor in a targeted community. In the aftermath of the July 15, 2016 coup attempt, in his attempts at unifying Turkey under his rule and neutralizing those perceived as his opposition, President Recep Tayyip Erdoğan has taken advantage of pre-existing conditions to scapegoat Hizmet/Gülen movement participants (as well as Kurds, Alevis, Leftists, and others), thousands of whom have fled Turkey. Blaming them for the failed putsch, he further ostracized them to the point that even casual participants have been fired from their jobs, rejected or reported by neighbors, friends, and family members, and even jailed and even tortured (Amnesty International, January 12, 2018).

According to the United Nations Universal Declaration of Human Rights (UNUDHR) (General Assembly Resolution 217 A), all people have the right to life, property, liberty, security of person, freedom from arbitrary arrest and torture, the right to work, the right to seek an education, the right to have freedom of movement among other things. The Turkish government has violated all of the above since 2016. Since then, women have been subjected to an ever-increasing number of intimidation strategies including rape, the threat of rape, harassment, and other forms of violence. These horrors are not only perpetrated by Erdoğan's AKP-led government, but also by civilians emboldened by the new climate in which macho hyper-masculinity and misogyny have become widespread. >>>

FREEDOM CONVENTION

FREEDOM CONVENTION

Not long after the putsch attempt, feminists noted an increase in attacks and harassment on the street. Journalist Pinar Ersoy writes that women have been "silenced" during the purge and that women's groups have been targeted.

In a Muslim, patriarchal country, an effective tactic to incite fear is to threaten the community's sense of honor. In general, Turkish men are tasked with protecting their wives and children; failing to do so is a dishonor. Many of the men interviewed wept when narrating their devastating inability to protect their wives during the purge. A recurring refrain was that they did not mind being arrested and even tortured themselves if it meant that their wives and children remain safe.

In February 2019, a Gülen movement-affiliated university student, Merve Demirel, took part in a peaceful protest and was sexually assaulted by a police officer (IPA News, 2019). The Ankara Police appeared to justify the assault by stating that "her father was a teacher who was dismissed from duty after the 2016 coup attempt", implying that her father was affiliated with the Gülen movement and thus deserved the dishonor of his daughter's assault (IPA News, 2019).

Women that are detained or jailed are vulnerable to strip searches, rape, and other demeaning treatment (Amnesty International, January 12, 2018). There are around 17,000 women currently jailed in Turkey.

A summary of the 2017 UN OHCHR report on Turkey states: "Turkish authorities reportedly detained some 100 women who were pregnant or had just given birth, mostly on the grounds that they were 'associates' of their husbands, who are suspected of being connected to the terrorist organizations. Some were detained with their children and others violently separated from them (OHCHR, 2017, p. 20).

Over 700 babies are held in jail with their imprisoned mothers in inadequate conditions (Turkish Minute, 2019). All of this violates the basic human rights to be free from arbitrary arrest,

> **Women have been subjected to an ever-increasing number of intimidation strategies including rape, the threat of rape, harassment, and other forms of violence. These horrors are not only perpetrated by Erdoğan's AKP-led government, but also by civilians emboldened by the new climate in which macho hyper-masculinity and misogyny have become widespread.**

unfair trials and detentions, torture, and "cruel, inhuman or degrading treatment or punishment." Article 25, in particular, notes that "motherhood and childhood are entitled to special care and assistance" (United Nations, 1948). Obviously, this has not been granted.

Scholars have written about the particular plight of women victimized by political conflict and their coping mechanisms, which include "external processes" such as accessing resources and "internal processes" such as reframing negative experiences, visualizing one's self in God's hands, and praying more. While those interviewed tend to tell me that prayer will heal them, it is unlikely that they will escape these wounds without earthly help as well, such as access to adequate basic resources (food, shelter) including mental health treatment.

Judith L. Herman (2015) argues that healing for the victims of collective violence begins when the violence against them is halted, their needs are provided for, and the perpetrators, as well as assenters of the atrocities, have been brought to justice. She also advocates that victims give testimony regarding their experiences, and find a "survivor mission" which can be sharpened by the traumatized group.

Until Erdoğan ceases his purge of the Gülen movement and removes the terrorist label he affixed to them, those with family members cannot safely speak out.

Those with privilege must speak for them.

FREEDOM CONVENTION

PROMOTING CIVIL AND POLITICAL RIGHTS

RUTH BEN-GHIAT

Ruth Ben-Ghiat is a historian and commentator on authoritarianism and propaganda. She is Professor of History and Italian Studies at New York University, the recipient of Guggenheim, Fulbright, and other fellowships, and Advisor to Protect Democracy. She is a regular contributor to CNN, MSNBC, and other media outlets. She publishes Lucid, a newsletter on threats to democracy. Her latest book, Strongmen: Mussolini to the Present (2020), looks at how illiberal leaders use propaganda, corruption, violence, and machismo – and how they can be defeated.

ERDOĞAN'S PERSONALITY CULT

I write about authoritarianism and how strongman leaders position themselves as saviors of the nation while using corruption, propaganda, virility, and repression in order to try and make themselves untouchable and above the law. I want to show how what has happened in Turkey, especially since the 2016 coup, conforms to this model. Understanding the strategies of legitimation helps us know how to push back against them.

Strongmen capitalize on the idea that they are bringing the nation to greatness. They channel three primary timelines: utopia, nostalgia, and crisis. Utopia, or the desire for a perfect national community, links to the leader's promise to make the country great. Often this is through modernization projects. So Erdoğan has been busy imprinting himself on the landscape, building airports, train stations, railways and highways, Kanal Istanbul on the Bosphorus, and more. This "progress" is often funded by foreign loans that leave the country in debt.

Nostalgia for a time of national grandeur is also key since the ruler vows to make the country great again. Mussolini had the Roman Empire, and Erdoğan has the Ottoman Empire - of course, a vision of an empire cleansed of the interfaith and interethnic exchange and cohabitation that made that empire such a cosmopolitan place. The hope of reviving the empire gives a rationale for any expansionist aims. New maps of Turkey that have appeared during the >>>

FREEDOM CONVENTION

FREEDOM CONVENTION

post-2016 coup attempt crackdown assert territorial claims in Greece and Iraq.

The most consequential time is crisis time, which justifies states of emergency and the scapegoating of enemies who endanger the country. It links to a conception of the state as an organic entity with the right to defend itself from threats to its safety, and of course, any attack on the leader is an attack on the nation as a whole.

And here we arrive at the importance of victimhood. Strongmen all pose as victims, and this victimhood complex is important to the appeal they have for their people. It is how they justify their attacks on the rule of law and human rights violations.

The coup attempt was a shock event that put Turkey into a crisis state, allowing Erdoğan to declare a state of emergency (which has continued on and off since then) so he could consolidate his power. Others have written about the terrible injustices that followed that July night: the purges that started with the army and continued with the Kurdish opposition, individuals associated with Gülen's Hizmet movement, and members of the judiciary, the press, academics, and more. The seizure of billions of dollars worth of businesses and other economic assets.

Here I want to talk about how Erdoğan used the cult of victimhood to come out of the coup attempt stronger. As is so often the case with strongmen, direct communication with the people at a fateful moment proved decisive. On the night of the coup, as rumors circulated that Erdoğan was dead or in exile, the President suddenly appeared on CNN Turk, speaking to the nation via FaceTime. CNN Turk anchor Hande Firat held her own iPhone and lapel microphone up to the camera. The sight of Firat's French-manicured fingers cradling his small image added to the sense of Erdoğan's vulnerability.

"We will overcome this," Erdoğan told the nation on television, using the first person plural to bond Turks to him. "Go to the streets... There is no power

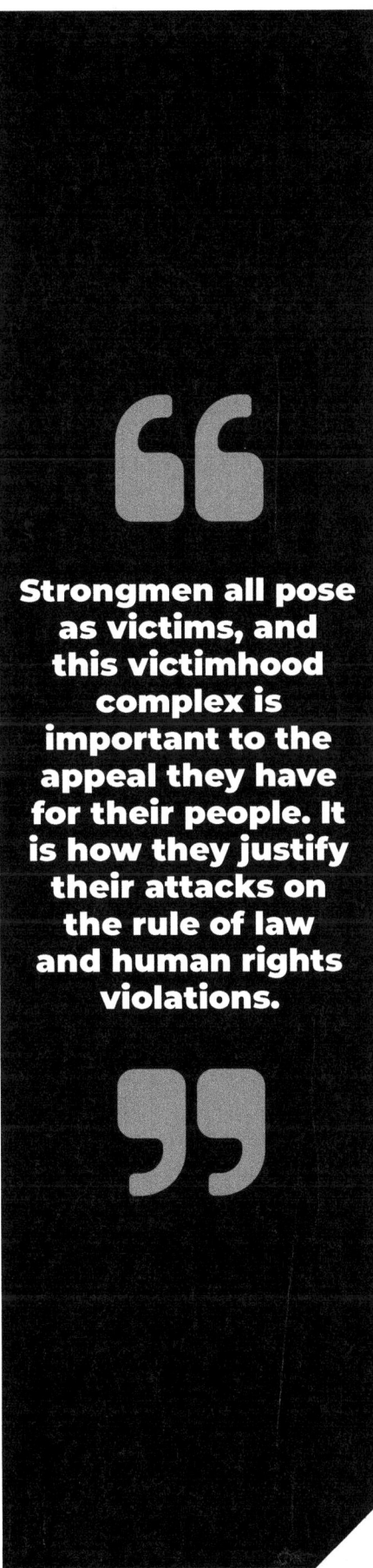

> **Strongmen all pose as victims, and this victimhood complex is important to the appeal they have for their people. It is how they justify their attacks on the rule of law and human rights violations.**

higher than the power of the people." His FaceTime call drew viewers into an unfolding saga that transcended party politics. A month after the coup, his approval ratings had risen from 50% to 70%. No wonder he declared the uprising "a gift from God" a few days later.

Predictably, the anniversary of the coup became an occasion to celebrate Erdoğan's survival and his ability to vanquish state enemies. As the coup attempt recedes in time the threat it commemorates must increase. In 2019, Erdoğan linked it to the West's attempt to "subject our nation to slavery." By then, he had been re-elected with expanded powers: since 2018 he has served as both President and Prime Minister.

I also want to mention two other aspects of Erdoğan's personality cult that play into these dynamics. First is his habit of crying in public. These tears are performative - as research by Semen Aslan has shown, they increase in frequency when his power is unstable. He cried 25 times in public after the 2013 Gezi Park protests and 18 times after the 2016 coup attempt. These crocodile tears, like his victimhood complex, show him to be "vulnerable" just when he is being more repressive.

Then there are the insult suits, the scale of which is staggering - more than 36,000 were people investigated in 2019 alone. Their psychological power lies in their randomness; since you can be targeted with no reason or evidence, you never know when it might happen to you. This promotes what all authoritarian states need in their people: self-censorship, silence, and fear. In the meantime, it keeps up the fiction that Erdoğan is constantly being attacked, criticized, and threatened.

I will continue to call public attention to the ways that Erdoğan uses classic strongman tactics to present himself as "good for business" and "good for the nation," while instead, he has acted in destructive ways, not least forcing so many talented professionals, including people at this event, to leave their homeland. We need to hear more about what is happening in Turkey, and I thank you for taking the time to sit with my thoughts. ■

FREEDOM CONVENTION

FREEDOM CONVENTION

ARBANA XHARRA

Arbana Xharra is an investigative journalist from Kosovo. She authored a series of investigative reports on religious extremists and Turkey's Islamic agenda operating in the Balkans. She has won numerous awards for her reporting and was a 2015 recipient of the International Women of Courage Award from the U.S. State Department.

I have been closely following the most ruthless dictator activities in the Balkans since 2012 – how they increased their influence gradually over the last decade, the methods they used to recruit different communities that are worshiping them. For those who don't know much about Kosovo, we have been under the terrible Serbian regime until 1999.

In the 90s, Europe and the U.S. provided shelter for hundreds of thousands of Albanians who resisted the tyrannical Milosevic regime. A few years later in 1999, the U.S., jointly with EU countries, launched NATO airstrikes against the Serbs' artillery position to end their atrocities. With the support of Western countries, Kosovo became the newest state in Europe. Kosovo is known as one of the most pro-American countries, where boulevards and streets are named after U.S. presidents. Kosovo is defined by its constitution as a secular state.

Now, Kosovo is being targeted by Turkey's President Erdoğan, who is bent on spreading his Islamic agenda throughout the Balkans. He views Kosovo as easy prey and a means by which to promote his wicked plans, and uses its submissive politicians to do his bidding.

In 2015, the daily newspaper Zeri revealed how Erdoğan is increasing his influence through building religious institutions, including dozens of new mosques, and the restoration of existing ones built during the Ottoman Empire.

Turkey's determination to invest in mosques is expanding Erdoğan's influence into other spheres as well. He has privatized the main Kosovo assets, Airport and Energy Distribution. Erdoğan replaced Albanian imams with his imams from Turkey. Religious structures have been financed through one large donor, the Turkish Cooperation and Coordination Agency (TİKA), which is directly managed by the Turkish embassy in Pristina.

For the last 10 years, he has invested in media as well. He is silencing critical voices via fake news. I face significant pressure every time I write against Erdoğan. Albanians must know that Erdoğan doesn't care about them, he wants to spread the Islamic agenda and threaten Europe by having influence in this very important part of Europe.

In March 2018, Kosovo deported six teachers from Gülen schools to Turkey, becoming the third country after Iraq and Sudan to hand Gülenists over to Erdoğan's brutal treatment. Erdoğan regularly pressures the EU and U.S. to deport "his enemies" to Turkey.

In 2018, during the election campaign, Erdoğan was banned from organizing events in EU countries, he went to Bosnia and addressed the Turkish diaspora. He uses Balkan countries for his own political agenda.

The influence of Erdoğan's Islamist agenda in Kosovo and other Balkan countries needs more scrutiny from Western countries. Erdoğan has already invested millions of dollars in mosques and other projects. Kosovo remains the only country in the Balkans deprived of visa liberalization, which isolates the country and increases the risk of creating a perfect atmosphere for Erdoğan's Islamic exploits.

> "Kosovo is being targeted by Turkey's President Erdoğan, who is bent on spreading his Islamic agenda throughout the Balkans. He views Kosovo as easy prey and a means by which to promote his wicked plans, and uses its submissive politicians to do his bidding."

FREEDOM CONVENTION

FREEDOM CONVENTION

MFANA GWALA

Adv. Mfana Gwala is an anti-apartheid activist in South Africa. He was recently appointed by the President of South Africa as a member of the Information Regulator South Africa. He is an executive member of the National Democratic Lawyers (NADEL) Bar Association with more than ten years of experience in public administration matters, employment and labor, constitutional litigation, procurement disputes, commercial litigation, and alternative dispute resolution. He has also served as an executive member of the Law Society of South Africa.

It is clear that the situation is very dire in Turkey. What attracted my attention the most was the presence of safeguards for both the judiciary and those who practiced law before the rule of Erdoğan. Internationally these safeguards are key to protecting human rights in any country. Dictators always target the independence of the judiciary and make sure that they staff courts with people who make decisions in their favor. They undermine the practice of law by controlling lawyers because lawyers, we know, are often the voice and the defenders of human rights.

I noticed that Turkey has a code that is regulated by Law number 1136. What is interesting about this code is that it basically makes it difficult or almost impossible to prosecute lawyers under normal circumstances. Erdoğan seems to be doing the exact opposite, ignoring this law altogether. There appears to be a systematic targeting of the judiciary system aimed at undermining its independence and frustrating the efforts of lawyers to represent their clients. From the reports that I've investigated, for example, about 1,600 lawyers have been arrested, some of them without trial, and only about 450 have been convicted via legitimate courts of law. The sentences for these individuals range from an average of about 15 to 20 years.

I lived in Apartheid South Africa. Even if being black in South Africa was a crime in and of itself, at least the Apartheid state created some semblance of mechanisms by which people could attempt to find some justice in court -

although in most cases the state would find a way to circumvent this process. For example, in the popular case of the Rivonia Trial of the former president Nelson Mandela and his comrades, there was a trial but all of us knew that that trial was a farce. But at least there was a trial. People were given an opportunity to publicly defend themselves. In Turkey, this seems to be non-existent.

The Erdoğan regime targets the sort of intelligence that can challenge his rule. I think you know that undermining the educated part of society makes it easy for him as a dictator to do as he pleases. I am quite impressed that in the midst of that, we still have things like the Turkey Tribunal in Geneva in September 2021. The composition of that Tribunal reminds me of the Cuban Five. Five people were arrested in America and branded as Cuban spies. They were sentenced to life in prison and some of them even to death. There was an international tribunal and among the judges, there was a judge from South Africa. That tribunal eventually found those people not guilty. I had the privilege of meeting the Cuban Five when they visited South Africa. What I am trying to say is that some of these instruments we may take for granted but they work.

We should not lose hope in these instruments, and I think it is important to also know that in South Africa, we relied heavily on international solidarity, on sanctions against the Apartheid government. A mass mobilization in South Africa also played a role. I was one of those people who were actively involved in the mass democratic movement, and it makes it easy to support other countries.

It seems that the system in Turkey was working well before the so-called coup. Things have gone south. If you look at what has happened - there are children in jail – at least in Apartheid South Africa, they respected the rights of children and, at times, women. They were still treated badly – but at least they tried not to >>>

> "Dictators always target the independence of the judiciary and make sure that they staff courts with people who make decisions in their favor. They undermine the practice of law by controlling lawyers because lawyers, we know, are often the voice and the defenders of human rights."

FREEDOM CONVENTION

FREEDOM CONVENTION

put children in jail. After everything that I have seen and been through, what is happening in Turkey still shocks me to my core.

Finally, what is also very shocking about what is happening in Turkey is that they don't just arrest lawyers, they even arrest leaders of the profession. I'm told that the presidents of the bar associations of Konya, Trabzon, and Gümüşhane were arrested. So it's quite clear that Erdoğan has identified the think-tank of the nation as the number one enemy to his rule. We need to continue to put pressure on the Turkish government to change its practices. I want to emphasize the point that it is through International solidarity that the Turkey issue can be resolved. We need to mobilize our people all over the globe. ■

THE CRACKDOWN ON RULE OF LAW

FREEDOM CONVENTION

FREEDOM CONVENTION

ARAT BARIŞ

Arat Barış, a journalist and an author, majored in International Trade and currently studies economics. He has written articles on politics and history for many different media outlets including Roj News, Democrat Haber, and Yön. He currently has a column at Dave, an online news portal. Barış also works on the issues of refugees, enforced disappearances and human rights violations in Turkey's jails.

The story that I'm about to tell may sound like a story from long ago, completely removed from our modern world, but this is neither a work of fiction nor something from the long-forgotten past, but a real story of people living today whose lives go on under the shadow of pain and torture. Every honest recounting of Turkey's recent history contains the shadows of those who have been made to disappear. Sometimes it is a child still growing into their potential, sometimes an old man with plenty of wisdom to share, or a young woman filled with hope and promise who falls victim to this atrocity. Sometimes a mother longing for her child or a father who is separated from his wife and children turns into a dark shadow on the list of those who have vanished.

This collection of shadows, called "unsolved" cases, is a picture of Turkey's suffering, but it also contains a clear expression of our human separation. It's very painful to express this, but ours is a society that "believes in the justification of death through the identity of the deceased." We're not concerned with the notion of death, but with who is dead. Instead of being a voice for those who were taken from their spouses, loved ones, and children, those who have disappeared and turned into a black shadow in the state records, we fight for and protect our in group, those who are close to us. We're not concerned with the pain of others, but with the part of the pain that touches us.

If the one who was disappeared or was murdered is not one of us, we ignore it and pretend like we do not know. Why this hypocrisy, this emptiness, and indifference to endless suffering? Is it the comfort of having a religion, even if we have no conscience? Or is it the embodiment of misery that does not feel ashamed to present their existence to the existence of the state?

At this point, what we need to question is not heaven, hell, or the sophisticated concepts of the modern age, but whether we're human. No more, no less... Because we're human to the extent that we feel the pain of others. And because we don't feel other pains equally, we're all a little flawed. Our priorities have never been "HUMAN", and because they haven't, we are always incomplete. Our love is incomplete, our dreams are incomplete, our smiles are incomplete.

At this point, what I have to say about the enforced disappearances and the sick prisoners in Turkey may sound unbelievable to you. Because, honestly, we're having trouble believing it. The recent history of Turkey is also a history of disappearances and unsolved murders. By holding sit-ins every Saturday since May 27, 1995, the Saturday Mothers have been asking for the truth about their relatives who disappeared in custody and were victims of unsolved political murders.

On January 8, 2020, Şimuni and Hurmüz Diril, a Chaldean couple, went missing in the village of Mehre in the Beytüşşebap district of Şırnak in southeastern Turkey. 70 days after their disappearance, on March 20, the couple's son Kemal found the lifeless body of his mother by chance on a 10-minute walk from their village. The fate of Hurmuz Diril is still unknown. Little attention has been given to the disappearance of this Chaldean couple because we were not concerned with the persecution and suffering of Şimuni and Hurmüz Diril, but with their identity - that they are Christians, in other words, not Muslims.

Gülistan Doku, a 2nd-year student in the Department of Child Development at Munzur University left her dormitory on the morning of January 5, 2020, and was never heard from again. There has been no news from the >>>

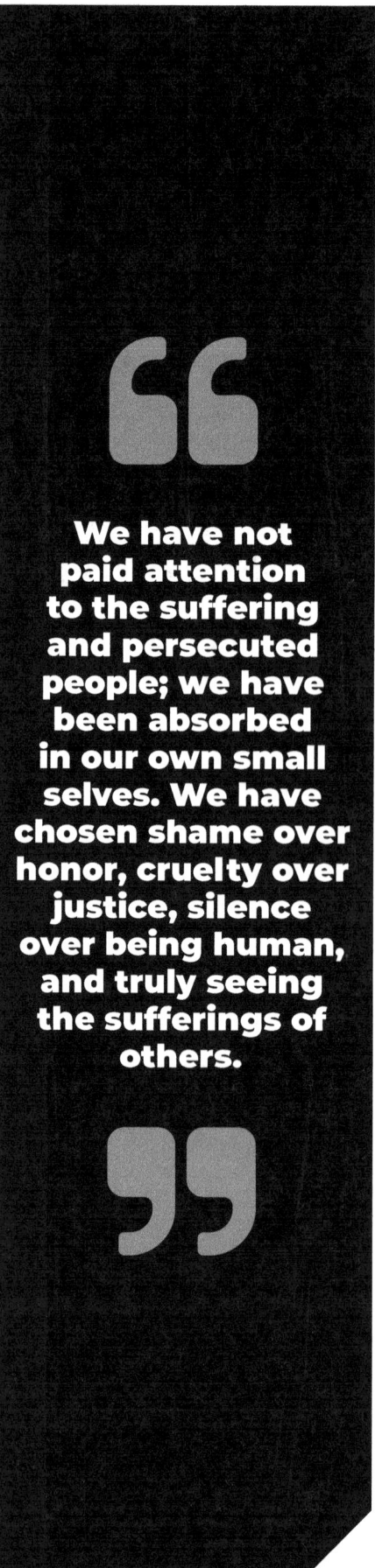

> We have not paid attention to the suffering and persecuted people; we have been absorbed in our own small selves. We have chosen shame over honor, cruelty over justice, silence over being human, and truly seeing the sufferings of others.

FREEDOM CONVENTION

FREEDOM CONVENTION

21-year-old woman for more than 700 days. And we were not concerned with the separation of a young girl from life, but with the fact that Gülistan Doku was from Diyarbakir and a Kurd.

Yusuf Bilge Tunç was expelled from his position at the Undersecretariat of Defense Industry by decree after the July 15 coup attempt. On August 6, 2019, he was abducted by a black van in the capital, Ankara. Since then, there has been no news of him for about 860 days. We were not concerned with the cries of his mother, who has been struggling and fighting to find her child, but with the ideological position of the family.

We have not paid attention to the suffering and persecuted people; we have been absorbed in our own small selves. We have chosen shame over honor, cruelty over justice, silence over being human, and truly seeing the sufferings of others. We have chosen to be the blind defenders of the state and its ideologies. As the poet said, "This is our crime deserving punishment."

On January 25, 2001, HADEP Silopi District President Serdar Tanış and District Secretary Ebubekir Deniz were summoned to the District Gendarmerie Command. They were never heard from again.

Everyone has something to say, something to cry out for, of course, but none of them has moved me in quite the same way as the cry of a child awaiting the return of their father. Ceylan Deniz, daughter of Ebubekir Deniz, who still dreams of the day her father will come, pulls on the heartstrings by saying that "It is very difficult to say, but even my father's bones will make us very happy now."

The presence of those who have vanished is like an ever-growing emptiness inside us. An emptiness where shadows roam and lament echoes. Instead of comforting the pain, we choose to run away. This choice does not save us, it just stifles our humanity, even as we try to protect ourselves.

Another open wound in Turkey is our sick prisoners. According to the Human Rights Association, there are a total of 1,605 inmates in Turkey's prisons, 604 of whom are seriously ill. One of them is Mehmet Emin Özkan. On October 22, 1993, Brigadier General Bahtiyar Aydın, regional commander of the Diyarbakır Gendarmerie, flew by helicopter to Lice district to lead the operation against the PKK. Brigadier General Aydın was shot dead by sniper fire as he got out of the helicopter in the military base in Lice. After Aydın was shot, the entrances and exits to the town were closed and an operation of massive scope was launched. During the three days of the operation, a sergeant and 14 civilians were killed and 650 houses and workplaces were destroyed. State officials at the time said the PKK carried out the attacks, while the residents of Lice, who were the victims of the incident, say security forces entered the town center and randomly set their houses and workplaces on fire.

After the assassination of Brigadier General Aydın, violence increased in Lice and mass migration began. Civilians from Lice migrated to Diyarbakır and western Turkey. Mehmet Emin Özkan, who was 57 at the time, was one of those who immigrated to Mersin.

Finding a job in Mersin province, Özkan's life was turned upside down

once again when he was detained in 1996. Özkan, who was accused of participating in the assassination of Aydın, was arrested, interrogated, and severely tortured. In his later statements, Özkan said he was illiterate and signed with his fingerprints many documents whose contents he did not understand. He was sentenced to life in prison with the testimonies of two confessors; however, the confessors later retracted their testimonies stating that they were taken under torture. Yes, a person's life was ruined based on testimonies that have been demonstrated to be false.

Özkan, aged 83, has been imprisoned for 26 years for an unproven crime. Despite more than 10 serious illnesses, he has still not been released.

As poet İlhan Çomak said: "Justice isn't being tried for a long, long time; justice is that the law applies to all; justice isn't to be imprisoned falsely; justice is not to be forgotten..." We're going through difficult times. It's dark where we live. We may feel trapped in a black hole, but we don't give up, because there's always a way out.

With that hope, I salute you all and wish for a better tomorrow.

FREEDOM CONVENTION

FREEDOM CONVENTION

SERDAR ÇELEBİ

Serdar Çelebi has been a lawyer registered in the Diyarbakır Bar Association for 16 years, where he also served as the chair briefly. He has worked for the Human Rights Organization (İHD) as assistant general director and branch director for a long time. Çelebi also worked on unsolved murder cases, mass graves of the victims of the Turkish regime, and inhumane jail conditions.

Ms. Aysel Tuğluk was elected as the first female party co-chair in the history of the Kurdish political party and is also the only female parliamentarian who was banned from politics with the closure of the Democratic Society Party (DTP). Tuğluk, who is also a lawyer and human rights defender, is a politician who has devoted her life to the struggle for freedom and equality of the Kurds, which will only find a final solution with an honorable peace.

As a result of the political operations that gained a new dimension with the arrest of HDP co-chairs, deputies, and co-mayors on November 4, 2016, Tuğluk was detained and arrested on December 25, 2016, while she was the deputy co-chair of Peoples' Democratic Party (HDP). The full case file on Tuğluk, who was sentenced to 10 years in prison for the (alleged) crime of forming or managing an organization with regards to the grounds that she participated in the activities of the Democratic Society Congress (DTK) and was the co-chairwoman of the DTK, is limited to her statements between 2011 and 2014. These statements are fully within the scope of constitutional political party activities and freedom of expression as an elected parliamentarian.

Tuğluk lost her mother in the early days of her incarceration. With special permission, she was allowed to leave the prison to attend the funeral. She was subjected to racist attacks during the funeral ceremony held in Ankara and the burial in the cemetery. Because of the organized racist attacks, the body of her 84-year-old mother was exhumed from the grave and taken to Dersim province for reburial. Tuğluk, who herself has been exposed to all this inhumane process, too, and who has paid a great price for years in Turkey's struggle for democracy, was seriously shaken after this attack at the funeral of her mom. This event, which led to serious questioning among all of those in Turkish society who were aware of such an inhumane process, left Tuğluk with irreparable, trauma-induced damage. This has only been aggravated with the effects of still being imprisoned and has now caused her serious health problems.

A report was unanimously issued by the Kocaeli Medical Faculty Forensic Medicine Board, indicating that she could not stay in prison due to her illness, which is progressing further and becoming more difficult to treat. However, despite this, the Istanbul Forensic Medicine Institute (ATK), which has for years been known for its reports that are not ethical, conscientious, scientific, or lawful, gave a report indicating that she could remain in prison, ignoring the report issued by the Kocaeli Medical Faculty Forensic Medicine Board. Although the report is contested, this is not the first report given by ATK. Despite the severe and deadly illnesses of political prisoners, the number of inmates who have died after repeated reports that "they can remain in prison", which are unscientific and unconscionable, continues to be quite high. It is important once again to draw attention to the fact that following the reports of human rights organizations that are issuing such reports on political prisoners is a common state policy.

Another discriminatory practice experienced by the inmates imprisoned for political reasons is that they are transferred to prisons far away from their families. Inmates who are transferred to places far from their residences are often unable to meet with visitors and lawyers due to distance and economic reasons. This is not only another punishment but also a serious violation of the right to defense. Relatives of inmates who visit the prison only a limited number of times due to economic difficulties are exposed to racist attacks and poor treatment, especially when they go to western prisons, >>>

> "Similar arbitrary punishments were also imposed in other prisons, without any legal justification, for songs sung in the Kurdish language, which they describe as an "unknown language"."

FREEDOM CONVENTION

FREEDOM CONVENTION

and may be exposed to the discriminatory practices and sometimes insults of some prison officers.

Although the intensity of persecution varies based on the political atmosphere, there are very serious pressures on the Kurdish language. Correspondence in Kurdish is denied on the grounds that there are no Kurdish translators in many prisons; sending letters in Kurdish is not allowed. Although singing songs in Kurdish is not a justification alone for disciplinary action, excuses - such as deeming songs sung in Kurdish as propaganda - are given as punishments are doled out to prisoners. As a matter of fact, Ms. Leyla Güven, who was arrested after being stripped of her parliamentary status, along with 13 other imprisoned female prisoners in Elazığ Women's Closed Prison was given a month-long communication punishment for singing and dancing in Kurdish. Similar arbitrary punishments were also imposed in other prisons, without any legal justification, for songs sung in the Kurdish language, which they describe as an "unknown language".

Similarly, critical newspapers like "Yeni Yaşam" and "Evrensel" are deemed as "forbidden publication" and are not delivered to inmates in prison. Furthermore, despite being published with the approval of the Ministry of Culture, many books containing "Kurdistan" are not given to prisoners on the grounds that they are banned publications. Kurdish books or poetry works owned by prisoners are arbitrarily seized during searches in many prisons and are not returned to them for months.

Another issue I would like to bring to your attention is the law on the execution of sentences applied to political

prisoners. In the law numbered 5275, it is regulated that persons convicted of organizational crimes who served three-quarters of their sentence and other inmates who serve two-thirds of their sentence in prison can be released conditionally. Although this distinction may seem like a "legal arrangement" at first, the definitions of crimes in the Turkish Penal Code, especially crimes such as membership in a terrorist organization and propaganda of such an organization, are not clear. Considering that we are in a period where it is very easy for people who express their thoughts or who use the democratic right to assembly and demonstration to be punished for being a member of an organization, it is clear that the law on execution of sentences also causes victimization. All the case files of the HDP deputies, who were sentenced after their immunity was unconstitutionally lifted in 2016, are limited to the speeches they gave while they were deputies and to the democratic marches they attended. Therefore, while a deputy, mayor, political party manager, human rights defender, or a member of an NGO are not released until they have served three-quarters of their sentence for expressing their thoughts, a person convicted of a criminal offense (such as theft, corruption) can be released after completing two-thirds of their sentence. Again, organizational crimes are excluded from the scope of the changes made in the execution law, which may be in favor of inmates. This not only goes against the principle of the equal protection of the law but also disrupts social peace.

Until 2021, the prisoner's attitudes and behaviors during their stay in prison were evaluated on the basis of whether there was a disciplinary penalty, but since 2021, prison administrations have made an unlawful decision that convicts staying in "ward for organized crimes" are denied benefiting from conditional release on the grounds that staying in the "ward for organized crimes" is an indication of not being "well-behaved". Yet all the prisons are controlled by the state, and as we have mentioned, prisoners are classified according to their crime types.

Again, the prisoners who have been "well behaved" while serving their sentence are asked if they regret their actions and they are forced to express regret in order to benefit from conditional release. Many of the prisoners we interviewed reacted to this by saying that "even though we are unjustly arrested and punished for exercising our constitutional rights, we are also forced to express regret."

As I have stated before, due to the unforeseen, unlawful consequences of the regulations in the penal code in Turkey (which resulted in violations of the ECHR for numerous convictions), many people are punished for membership in a "terrorist" organization because of their opinions and because they exercise their right to organize, assemble and demonstrate. These are far from being a crime in a democratic society. The personal rights of those who have been unjustly punished and imprisoned for years for expressing their opinions are also violated as they are forced to express regret. The current executions of the law leads to political prisoners not even benefiting from the written law and spending their entire sentence in prison against the written code.

FREEDOM CONVENTION

YASEMİN MAMALOĞLU

Born and raised in Germany, Yasemin Mamaloğlu majored in Mathematics and Law, mastered in Law. She lives with her 3 children and husband in Toronto, Canada.

What I am going to talk about today is neither a story nor fiction. It was truly what I personally experienced. I am a former high school math teacher of over 20 years and a lawyer now living in Toronto. Turkey progressed as a democratic country until December 2013. Erdoğan was the prime minister at that time. Due to heroic and capable police and prosecutors revealing his corruption, Erdoğan launched a perception operation on people who are virtuous and critical of him. When referring to us he used the term "hashashi," a deviant sect, members of which were opium addicts and assassinated people hundreds of years ago. Between 2013 and 2016 it worked. Schools were shut down, cops, judges, prosecutors were put in prisons and a lot of companies were confiscated by the AKP regime. However, it wasn't enough for Erdoğan. People who express their opinions freely annoyed him.

Since the failed, fabricated coup on July 15, 2016, more than 500,000 people, men, and women, have been detained and approximately 100,000 have been arrested. My husband, who was a judge, was put in jail for a year and a half and I was put in jail for two and a half years (as if I was a big and dangerous terrorist). Just one month before the 15th of July, almost 4,000 judges and prosecutors were exiled to different places of duty. We were among them. A friend of ours (a prosecutor) complained regarding this situation to a judge, Basri Bağcı, who is a current member of the Constitutional Court. His response was remarkable due to the date (only one month before July 15, 2016). He said "don't worry. If you don't want to go, you shouldn't. In any case, you will be fired from your job."

We, therefore, knew that something would go wrong, but we couldn't have predicted this. We were at a picnic when the failed, fabricated coup attempt happened in Turkey. We got the first information over the phone. Then we drove home very worried. Erdoğan gave a statement, which included information about the perpetrators. He said members of the Hizmet movement were to blame, calling them terrorists. They don't deserve anything like that, which impacts even their spouses, children, mothers, and fathers.

Merely 2-3 hours later, a list was released regarding judges and prosecutors who were fired without any investigation. Erdoğan and his advocates, judges, prosecutors, and cops interoperated and arrested hundreds of thousands of people. Eventually, on that night 2,745 members of the judiciary were arrested for a failed, fabricated coup. In just 2-3 hours, how can they decide almost 3,000's guilt? With a maximum of three hours, there was not enough time to sign the expulsion list. This was explicit evidence that thousands of members of the judiciary were innocent. Our colleagues and their spouses were arrested without any legal trial. Here are some of the questions prosecutors were asking while taking statements:

- What is the name of the school your children attend?
- Have you ever attended FETO's schools or dorms?
- Did you read FETO's newspapers?

What is even more interesting is that all prosecutors in Turkey ask the same questions. Furthermore, all the plaintiff's records of testimony have the same questions and grammatical errors. In one night, 13 judges and prosecutors were arrested while in my apartment, despite law number 2802. According to Article 88 of this law, judges and prosecutors who are alleged to have committed crimes, except for cases of flagrante delicto that fall under the jurisdiction of the heavy penal court, cannot be interrogated or taken in, their bodies and residences cannot be searched. However, they destroyed the law.

I would like to share some names of the members of the judiciary, who eviscerated the law on that day in Konya.

- Harun Can - Currently members of the supreme court
- Ersin Berber - Currently prosecutor
- Hayriye Aydogdu - Currently judge
- Melike Tanagirdi - Judge
- Hüseyin Topçuoğlu - Prosecutor
- Bestami Tezcan - Attorney General

I also want to talk about the mothers in the jail. Jail is already difficult for innocent people, but for women, especially for mothers, it is much worse. Kissing, smelling, hugging children is a natural action for mothers; however, a mother in a prison doesn't have the luxury of doing that. When they dreamed of having children, it was nothing like this. There is no one to pick up when they fall. They always have to be strong.

Another trauma for mothers has to do with the visiting time. The right to visit face to face and behind the glass communications were arbitrarily restricted. Visit days were changed from once a week to once every two weeks. Those who do not comply with these rules are banned by the administration of jail. There are no clocks in their room and they didn't give any warning that the visit is almost over. Suddenly they turn off the electricity and they start to shout. >>>

FREEDOM CONVENTION

As a mother, you must push your children! Yes, you must push children without hugging, kissing, or smelling!

I added up the time which I shared with my children while I was in prison for two and a half years. It was less than 24 hours. Less than a day. Food wasn't enough and also it smelled disgusting. I want to give a very simple example: we couldn't eat pasta without first washing it. Yes it sounds strange, but we had to wash it if we wanted to eat it. Although there were 20 women in the ward, they brought us only 3 potatoes. How could twenty women share only three potatoes?

Although criminal offenders had the right to give gifts to their children, we didn't have equal rights like them. As I remember accurately, in March of 2017, some guards, a principal, and doctors came to our ward and without any explanation, they vaccinated us forcibly. When we wanted information about what it was, they didn't say anything. Furthermore, they insulted us as usual.

> **Finally, when the courageous police officers were arrested in December of 2013 by the Erdoğan regime and the members of the judiciary loyal to him, I swore that I would stand up for human rights and democracy until the bitter end.**

I want to mention a little about my case too, because I want to make public the names of the prosecutors and judges who were like tyrants and acted illegally, not implementing the laws properly. Nevzat Sargın was my first prosecutor. When I was giving my statement at the police station, he contacted the cops there and had parts of my statements regarding Harun Can, a member of the Supreme Court at the moment, removed.

Beyhan Berber arrested me without any evidence and Mustafa Özden prepared my indictment. Our sons were in the same school, which was known as the Hizmet movement's school. If sending children there is a crime, why is he still on duty? The answer is so simple because they owe allegiance to dictator Erdoğan. Eyüp Mergen unfairly sentenced me to 8 years and 3 months in prison for his prejudices. He is currently a member of the Supreme Court.

To sum all of this up, judges and prosecutors, who have made decisions and signed statements or issued verdicts illegally, will stand before a tribunal soon. They have no excuse because they have made their decisions intentionally. I hope God gives me a chance to judge them as soon as possible.

Finally, when the courageous police officers were arrested in December of 2013 by the Erdoğan regime and the members of the judiciary loyal to him, I swore that I would stand up for human rights and democracy until the bitter end. That's why, even though I can't do anything right now, this attitude is very valuable and very important to me.

I would like to thank my mom and dad for raising me ethically and morally, to thank my children and my husband for always supporting me, as well as our friends. I am proud of all of them, who didn't sell their honor.

FREEDOM CONVENTION

DISCRIMINATORY GOVERNMENT POLICIES AGAINST MINORITIES, ETHNICITIES, DISSIDENTS

DAVID PHILLIPS

David L. Phillips is Director of the Program on Peace-building and Rights at Columbia University's Institute for the Study of Human Rights. Phillips has served as Foreign Affairs Expert and as Senior Adviser to the U.S. Department of State and as Senior Adviser to the United Office for the Coordination of Humanitarian Affairs. Phillips has been a Senior Fellow at Harvard University's Future of Diplomacy Project and Fellow at Harvard University's Center for Middle East Studies.

US officials often talk about restoring democracy in Turkey. Under Kemal's rule, Turkey was never a democracy. Its abuse of Kurds and Christian minorities, including genocide of Armenians, dates back to the waning years of the Ottoman Empire and the founding of the Republic of Turkey.

US officials initially welcomed the AKP's rise in 2002. They hoped that its rise would bring democracy. It was wishful thinking. Erdoğan was never a "democrat" or secular. In his speech given in Siirt in 1998, he said: "The mosques are our barracks, the domes our helmets, the minarets our bayonets and the faithful our soldiers." He was sentenced to 6 months in jail for using religion to foment divisions. After AKP won the 2002 elections, Erdoğan pronounced: "Democracy is like a streetcar. You get off when you've reached your destination."

The deterioration in US-Turkey relations accelerated in May 2013 after the crackdown of protesters in Gezi Park. Police brutality spread to 60 cities. Concerns about freedom of expression intensified. Article 8 of the Anti-Terror Act and Article 301 of the Penal Code are used to restrict freedom of expression. Article 301 makes it a crime "to denigrate Turkishness"

Turkey's Islamism and complicity with ISIS became a major concern. Secretary of State Hillary Clinton lamented Turkey's "new more serious Islamic reality". She decried Saudi Arabia and Emiratis' support of Turkey. U.S. officials also condemned Turkey's ties to jihadi organizations including ISIS.

During a speech at Harvard on 10/3/2014, Biden said: "Our allies in the >>>

FREEDOM CONVENTION

FREEDOM CONVENTION

region were our largest problem in Syria. The Turks were so determined to take down Assad and essentially have a Sunni-Shiite proxy war, they poured hundreds of millions of dollars, thousands of tons of weapons to anyone who would fight against Assad. Erdoğan admitted, 'You are right, we let too many of them through'." 40,000 foreign fighters from 80 countries made their way through Turkey to the frontline in Syria. Their engagement was facilitated by Turkey's National Intelligence Agency – systematically and deliberately. The jihadi highway ran from Şanlıurfa to Raqqa.

Relations further deteriorated when Erdoğan accused the U.S. of complicity in the July 15, 2016 coup. Tens of thousands were arrested and 150K were dismissed from their jobs. Erdoğan accused Fethullah Gülen of organizing the coup. I don't know anything about that. I do know that Gülen and Erdoğan were partners and the Gülen movement is as undemocratic and hostile to human rights as the AKP. For the record, I have no favor or ties to the Gülen movement.

I do stand with the people of Turkey whose rights have been systematically denied by the AKP. U.S. officials criticized Turkey for adopting its new constitution on 4/16/2017, which transformed its parliamentary system into a presidential one. The Venice Commission said it was "a dangerous step backwards, putting Turkey on the path to authoritarianism."

Erdoğan's decision to acquire S-400 missiles at a cost of $2.5 billion was strongly criticized by the US, leading to Turkey's exclusion from the F-35 stealth bomber weapons system. As a NATO member, Turkey knows the core principle of interoperability between weapons systems.

US-Turkey relations deteriorated further when Turkey joined the Astana process, an alternative to UN mediation that also involved Russia and Iran.

No issue has polarized U.S.-Turkey relations more than U.S. security cooperation with Kurds in Syria and Iraq. The Syrian Democratic Forces

> US officials initially welcomed the AKP's rise in 2002. They hoped that its rise would bring democracy. It was wishful thinking. Erdoğan was never a "democrat" or secular.

(SDF), led by General Mazloum Kobani, includes Syrian Kurds at its core. Though 40% of PKK members come from Syria, Syrian Kurdish groups are operationally distinct from the PKK. Rojava, a region in North and East Syria where Kurds predominate, is a model of grassroots democracy, women's empowerment, and environmental sustainability inspired by Öcalan's views on democratic federalism.

FAILURE TO SUPPORT THE KURDS

Kobani, a small city in Syria on its Turkish border, was the turning point. It was attacked by ISIS in September 2014. ISIS was supplied by Turkey and launched attacks from the hills of Suruc. Their collusion was well documented by Cumhurriyet, and Can Dündar, the editor in chief, was jailed for revealing state secrets.

Initially, U.S. officials including ex-ambassador Ryan Crocket believed "we don't have a dog in this fight", but the prospects of Kobani's heroic defenders being overrun and beheaded compelled the U.S. to take action. It airlifted weapons and medical supplies enabling Kurdish forces to push ISIS out after 4 months of fighting. Kurds proved their mettle in Kobani.

The Pentagon needed boots on the ground to fight ISIS and supported the YPG with weapons and airpower as it pivoted East, attacking Tal Abyad on the Turkey-Syria border. In August 2016, the SDF ousted the FSA from Mambij. In May 2017, the SDF captured Raqqa. 6,000 ISIS were killed in brutal hand-to-hand fighting.

US support for the Kurds was tactical. While supporting Kurds on the battlefield, the U.S. acceded to Turkey's demand and barred Kurds in the PYD from attending diplomatic meetings in Geneva unless they joined the delegation of the Syrian Opposition Council. Salih Moslem, PYD co-chair, applied for a U.S. visa at the embassy in Stockholm and received no reply.

The SDF is the tip of the spear fighting ISIS. Erdoğan was outraged when Secretary of State Rex Tillerson announced a Border Security Force including 40,000 YPG to guard against incursions by ISIS from Turkey. Erdoğan threatened to strangle the baby before it was born.

December 2017: Trump tells Erdoğan that the U.S. will withdraw. Sec Def Jim Mattis and Special Envoy Brett McGurks resign.

January 20, 2018: Turkey launched cross-border operations targeting Afrin. A woman and her daughter were hit by a missile and the girl was blown to bits. The mother was left holding the girl's arm, all that was left of the child.

After this Turkey established so-called safe zones in Northern Syria purging the area of Kurdish civilians and compelling the SDF's withdrawal. This practice of ethnic cleansing is ongoing.

September 2019: Erdoğan announced that 3 million refugees would return to the de-escalation zone on the Syrian side of the border. Forced repatriation violates international norms requiring "safe, orderly and dignified return". When the UN launched a constitutional committee in June 2018, Turkey unabashedly took steps to influence the selection of its members and its agenda.

October 6, 2019: Trump and Erdoğan had a phone call. Trump declared >>>

FREEDOM CONVENTION

FREEDOM CONVENTION

America's retreat from North and East Syria. Erdoğan didn't wait this time. Turkey Invaded on the 9th, occupying the area between Tal Abyad and Ras al Ain (Serekaniye).

December 2019: Trump announced 2000 U.S. Special Forces will leave Syria. Later he backtracked, saying that 400 would remain to prevent the resurgence of ISIS. In response Sen. Mitt Romney said: "The U.S. betrayal of the SDF is a bloodstain on America's reputation. Trump abandoned the SDF, America's best and only friend in Syria. The SDF lost 11K killed and 23k seriously injured fighting ISIS at our behest."

CONCLUSION

After America's retreat from Afghanistan, Syrian Kurds feared that the Biden administration would cut and run, leaving them to reprisals by Turkey and jihadist forces. Ilham Ahmed, President of the Executive Committee of the Syrian Democratic Council, met U.S. officials in late September 2021 to discuss continued cooperation between U.S. Special Forces and the YPG/YPJ. She was assured that the U.S. deployment in Syria would continue in order to destroy the Islamic State, build infrastructure, and remain a player in pursuit of a political solution.

Biden's Executive Order 13894 indicated "the actions by the Government of Turkey to conduct a military offensive into northeast Syria, undermines the campaign to defeat the Islamic State of Iraq and Syria, or ISIS, endangers civilians, and further threatens to undermine the peace, security, and stability in the region, and continues to pose an unusual and extraordinary threat to the national security and foreign policy of the United States. Therefore, ... I am continuing for 1 year the national emergency declared in Executive Order 13894 with respect to the situation in and in relation to Syria."

US officials always told me that faced with a decision between Turkey and the Kurds, the U.S. would always choose Turkey. Is that still the case? U.S. diplomacy should focus more on advancing the interests of its friends and allies and less on placating its adversaries.

Turkey has gone rogue. Steely-eyed realism is needed to see Turkey as it is, not how it may have been or we wish it to be. ■

MELTEM ARIKAN

Meltem Arıkan is a Turkish/Welsh author, known for her sharp critique of society and fearless and outspoken voice in her novels, plays, poems and articles. Her novel Yeter Tenimi Acıtmayın (Stop Hurting My Flesh) was banned in early 2004 by the Committee to Protect Minors from Obscene Publications. The ban was lifted after a legal fight and Arıkan was awarded the "Freedom of Thought and Speech Award 2004" by the Turkish Publishers' Association. She has received several awards and was short-listed for the "Freedom of Expression Award" in 2014 by Index on Censorship for her play Mi Minor.

I once wrote an absurd play. My life story has surpassed that fictional absurdity.

In 2004, the government banned my fourth book "Stop Hurting My Flesh." When they banned my novel, I felt pure fury. After that, I started a lot of campaigns, one of which was to have the word "incest" be accepted. Before my book, if you said the word "incest" on TV, you would be fined, but the act of incest itself was not punished at all. And you couldn't open a case on incest because there were no laws against it. The closest one pertained to child abuse, but these are totally separate matters. My campaigns contributed to the word being accepted. And the law changed.

Later, I was awarded the 'Freedom of Thought and Speech Award' by the Turkish Publishers Association, but my fury still grew. And then it occurred to me that we face a much larger issue; people are actually comfortable with the way things are. And people like to be comfortable. When I would bring up an uncomfortable topic, people thought me paranoid or histrionic, so I stopped.

When Wikileaks published the data cables, it flipped the male-dominated world order on its head. Seeing that leaders were powerless against Wikileaks from fearlessly publishing data cables excited me very much. The Turkish press did not pay enough attention to what was happening around the world. That's why I started to follow the developments from the world press and social media. I used my Facebook and Twitter ▶▶▶

FREEDOM CONVENTION

FREEDOM CONVENTION

accounts to inform the people in my country about world events. I was not interested in social media much before, but afterward, I spent most of my time sharing information. I became obsessed. People even wrote tweets saying, 'have some sleep; you need to sleep'. But I wanted to be awake when people started tweeting in the U.S. due to the time difference.

For two years, around the time of Arab revolutions and the Occupy movement, I felt, received, and perceived what was happening worldwide via social media. I witnessed how social media offered a platform for people to share their personal stories or provide information. People would broadcast with their phones using Ustream and live-stream when traditional media fell silent. After I got involved in social media, I didn't care about individual countries anymore because I realized that interactions on social media happen regardless of the borders of distances, languages, nations, religions, or ideologies. This inspired me to create a play. It was all about the situations and events happening all around the world. Later, I shared the script of Mi Minor with people from various countries. A friend from the U.S. read my play and said, "this is just like the U.S". Then during the rehearsals, a friend said that it resembles Korea, and another said it was just like Turkmenistan. This was exactly what I wanted, that it was perceived by a diverse group of people as their own country.

As a writer, it felt essential to understand what kind of a change was happening, to see the free flow of information and how people's perception was changing. During that time, I realized we were transitioning from the analog to the digital world. And I was interested to see how the perception was changing, especially to see where young people's worldview was heading and how it affected the relationship between people and government. As a woman and writer, not just using social media, but becoming aware of the kind of impact it has had and using it to develop an art piece to make others aware of the transition we are in – all this has changed my life completely.

Mi Minor [my play] was staged in İstanbul from 1 December 2012 to 14 April 2013. The play was performed 23 times, and more than 10,000 people attended. Gezi Park protests started on the 27th of May and on the 10th of June, the pro-government newspaper Yeni Şafak came out with the headline, "What A Coincidence", accusing Mi Minor as being the rehearsal for the protests, six months in advance. The subtitle said, "New information has come to light to show that the Gezi Park protests were an attempted civil coup." They continued by claiming that "the protests were rehearsed months before in the play called 'Mi Minor' staged in İstanbul".

After the Yeni Şafak headline, the mayor of Ankara started to make programs on TV specifically about Mi Minor mentioning my name. Once the premise of the conspiracy was established, any figure who somehow participated in the protests would always be linked to it, and thus to the foreign governments. I was shocked when I read the accusations in pro-government newspapers and saw it taken to the extreme on TV. In my play, I intended to criticize the patriarchy and perception of the analog world. Even though all the countries in the world are being ruled by different leaders, even though it seems like every country has a different system of its own, I believe the

Patriarchy holds similar dominance everywhere. When I was researching for Mi Minor [in 2011] I did everything I could so that the play wasn't associated with Turkey, Turkish politics, or any other actual country. It created a fictional dystopia. Mi Minor is an absurd play and it scares me that it could be accused of being responsible for what happened in Gezi Park.

The most troubling part is that these accusations are ongoing. In 2019 the Turkish court accepted the Gezi Indictment seeking life sentences for 16 people, including me. I wrote an absurd play and now my life has become more absurd than my play. One of the icons of Gezi Park demonstrations being the woman in red dress and the revolutionary pianist with the red dress in my play Mi Minor is a coincidence.

To be honest, even now, I don't want to remember what I went through during those days. I was extremely distressed. I received hundreds of threats and accusations every minute on social media. Mi Minor was discussed on TV channels at least twice a week. I started to use antidepressants because it felt impossible to understand and cope with what was going on. I wasn't just worried for myself but also for the people I love.

The arrests and accusations continued. We were prepared for every possibility, including my own arrest. It was nerve-wracking to live with such uncertainty. All this happened because I attended a peaceful protest to protect trees and then created a play.

I'M GUILTY, I CONFESS

I'm guilty; as a woman writer, for years I've been rejecting the male-dominated system. I've spent the last couple of years trying to interpret and communicate what's been happening during the transition from an analog to a digital world. I confess; two and a half years ago, using my intellect and my imagination, I wrote a play called "Mi Minor". Our play was performed 23 times in 3 different venues with the permission of the Governorship of İstanbul for each venue. My imagination fails me when I try to understand those who accuse >>>

> It's women and men that create cultures and civilizations. It is a big mistake to restrict the parameters of cultural formation just with race, religion, geography, and traditions, separate from the existence of women and men.

FREEDOM CONVENTION

FREEDOM CONVENTION

us of rehearsing the Gezi Park events before it has started, provoking all that is currently happening in our country; linking us to various foreign organizations and part of a fantastical conspiracy theory relating to all these lies – even though they haven't seen our play. I'm guilty; I know that for thousands of years fear culture has been creating 'the other' through racial and religious differences and making up rational reasons for wars by imposing hate and violence. I say ENOUGH to the analog world order imposed by the male-dominated system based on the culture of fear, which is the one and only common culture of all societies in the world and which has been forced upon all societies, for thousands of years.

I confess; culture shall not be attributed to any society or any race. Culture is formed through the results of women and men's existence(s) affecting each other and their interactions with nature. When defining cultural differences, the analog world order has always disregarded the differences between the lives of men and women, which forms the foundation of all cultures. It's women and men that create cultures and civilizations. It is a big mistake to restrict the parameters of cultural formation just with race, religion, geography, and traditions, separate from the existence of women and men.

I believe the new digital order will be constructed by accepting that societies are formed by women and men without prioritizing race, religion, language, and sexual differences.

I'm guilty; I believe in freedom of thought and freedom of expression by getting away from the pressures of all ideologies, political statements, military or civilian coups.

I confess; I want to think and live freely by moving away from the thought patterns that have been imposed by the patriarchal system for thousands of years.

I'm guilty; I know that the only reason for running away from reality, deflecting reality, creating 'the other' is fear. I confess; I will not be frightened and become 'the other'." ∎

BÜŞRA NİSA SARAÇ

Büşra Nisa Saraç is a PhD candidate at the University of Portsmouth, UK. Her work focuses on understanding the representation of Yazidi women's experiences under ISIS rule. Her research interest lies in exploring the intersections of security, gender-based violence, and the media.

I would first like to set the scene for our broader discussion on government policies. I am going to briefly talk about two case studies of violence perpetrated by state actors and non-state actors through a gender perspective. The first case study I would like to talk about is Yazidi women. Yazidis are a religious minority and were persecuted by the so-called Islamic State in 2014. The Yazidi community was subjected to gender-based violence. In many accounts, ISIS murdered 3,100 men first after they refused to convert to Islam, then kidnapped more than 5,000 women and girls and displaced the entire population from their ancestral homeland. Many women live in displaced camps in the Kurdistan region of Iraq, which represents the long-term implications of gender-based violence for this ethnic minority group.

Moving on the second case study, which is more related to this panel, is the women of Turkey.

Gender and sexuality issues have long been topics of discussion in Turkey's fragile political context. Long before the AKP came to power in 2002, women's bodies, sexuality, and their rights have been objects of debate in Turkey's political history. Since the foundation of the Turkish Republic, gendered and sexualized narratives were used by both the defenders of secular state ideology and political Islam to position themselves in relation to specific political events.

More recently, however, the discourses of the current ruling party had excited many citizens from different political backgrounds because they had concentrated on gender-sensitive laws, which represented important improvements in terms of women's subordination. For instance, with the amendment of the Penal code in 2004, punishments for gender-based violence increased; in line with the Istanbul >>>

FREEDOM CONVENTION

Convention signed in 2012, Turkey passed laws that aimed to prevent violence against women.

These developments were seen as progressive and positive steps towards the elimination of violence against women. Nonetheless, the AKP made a U-turn, fell short of substantially addressing gender-based inequality, discrimination based on sexual orientation, and withdrew from İstanbul Convention in 2021. With that, discourses and policies have taken an increasingly oppressive turn. As the AKP government grew increasingly authoritarian, people of different ideological and political backgrounds have been subjected to different forms of systematic and social violence and gender and sexuality issues have been one of the areas in which the oppressive turn manifested itself with growing levels of persecution and unjust incarceration of women in Turkey.

> **As the AKP government grew increasingly authoritarian, people of different ideological and political backgrounds have been subjected to different forms of systematic and social violence and gender and sexuality issues have been one of the areas in which the oppressive turn manifested itself with growing levels of persecution and unjust incarceration of women in Turkey.**

ANJEL DIKME

Anjel Dikme is an author and radio broadcaster. She has written articles in many different art and politics magazines including Newroz. She also authored the book "Kimlik Istemem" meaning I don't want an identity. Her son, Anjel Dikme currently lives in Paris.

There is a phrase I come across very often on social media: "Let's leave the past in the past, let's look at the present." But I want to tell you that what we call the past has never actually passed, it is always here, in the present. Today there is always a demand for justice. I am here because of what I see when I look at Turkey. It seems that I have to tell it again and again. I wrote a book, wrote articles, and did radio broadcasting for 19 years. I thought it would reach everyone when I told the truth, but it didn't. When I watch how 100-year, 150-year-old lies poison society, when I see these tyrants at work – which is the tactic of Goebbels, Hitler's propaganda minister – it seems that the more you repeat the lie, the more convincing it will be. Unfortunately, this is what has happened in our country since the Ottoman period.

When I saw this truth, I said, "How naive have you been, Anjel". That's why I'm here today. As defenders of truth, as the tellers of truth, we have to tell them over and over again. I will tell my own story, set out from there, and try to explain to you why the country has become the way it is today.

My father's side is from Sason, I myself am from Diyarbakır. You know in Turkey, what is said about the Armenians is that they are traitors and rebels. Why did they want to leave the Ottoman Empire? I'll offer a few examples as to why they were passed down in my own family. I knew that there were two women kidnapped from my family during the Republican period. Talking to my cousins while working on my second book, I learned that there was a third woman. A mother of three, this woman was kidnapped by a Kurdish agha [a tribe leader] and her husband committed suicide because his wife has been kidnapped. In the Republican era, her husband could not go and seek justice, he could not say "they kidnapped my wife", >>>

FREEDOM CONVENTION

FREEDOM CONVENTION

instead he hung and killed himself. Then there was the first night right, which was practiced in certain regions. They used to say "if the agha [regional leader] is cruel, life will be very difficult. But if he is a merciful agha, we will live very well." In other words, there was pain in direct proportion to what the agha was like.

The right of the first night was the practice of a bride spending her wedding night in the bed of the agha. I talked about this with a Kurdish friend recently, who is also a writer. I said, "I think Kurdish women have also been exposed to this because they were like the slaves of the aghas in Kurdish society. I'm sure there are Kurdish women who experienced this, not just Christians, Armenians." He went and asked his mother about it. His mother said, "How could the Armenians allow such a thing?" I was also very surprised when I first learned about it, but we learn from reading about the conditions of that period. In the Ottoman Empire it was forbidden for Christian subjects to hold a gun and ride a horse. Think

> **I do not think that there is a greater crime, sin, violation of law, or violation of rights than the lies that these tyrants and states tell people. Because, with these lies, they are so corrupting in society that I can't see a greater crime. Indeed the common denominator of all these violations we have talked about is "lie".**

about it, if they couldn't snatch the bride away by bullying with a mafia-like structure, they murdered the family. These women have been subject to this rape for centuries to protect their families. Can you imagine?

I especially want to ask the gentlemen, those who call these people traitors, please think. If your governor, your mayor, or your local official said "that new bride will go through my bed first", how would you react to this? Who says "yes" to that? When they say no, shall we call them traitors? Shall we call them heroes? I want you to ask yourselves this question. Justice is very important.

Secondly, another reason for the rebellion was taxes. Christian subjects paid a tax to stay in their religion, to live their faith. The Ottomans already collected a tax from them and then another for their faith. On top of that they also paid a tribute to the Kurdish landlords in their region. If they didn't pay this tribute they had no chance to live. So they said "enough is enough" in the face of this cruelty for centuries. Finally, they sent news to the sultan, "Enough, my sultan, let's pay taxes to you or to the aghas." They say that Armenians were rich; that is also a big lie. The Armenian bourgeoisie existed, but the Armenian people were largely peasants. My father was a shepherd, he was a beekeeper in the mountains. These people were farmers.

Why am I telling you all this? When I look at the country today, what I see does not surprise me; I am very sad but not surprised. When you know what happened in the past, it is easy to see that this is a continuation. If the screams of those Armenian women had been heard, if a just society had been built at that time, would so many women be dying today? No one would be able to kill people and freely roam the streets. We are talking about human rights. Ever since I was invited to share my thoughts on this panel, I've been thinking about what the biggest human rights violation is. I do not think that there is a greater crime, sin, violation of law, or violation of rights than the lies that these tyrants and states tell people. Because, with these lies, they are so corrupting in society that I can't see a greater crime. Indeed the common denominator of all these violations we have talked about is "lie".

Equality and justice have been what the Armenians wanted ever since the Ottoman era. Read the social movements, the statutes of their parties. Read the parliamentary speeches like the ones by Krikor Zohrab, who was a deputy back in those days. Read Paramaz's speeches before he was hanged along with twenty young people who were hanged in Beyazıt, Istanbul. Now look back to today; nothing has changed. Look, Rabia Naz's father is being treated like a madman today because he demands justice for his murdered daughter. Saturday Mothers have been attempting to claim their children's missing bodies since 1995. There are so many examples, I will not go here one by one and take your time. All this is because we never achieved justice in 1915, so we're stuck here. For example, if there was a justice mechanism for minority individuals who were fired from jobs or expelled from the country just because they were non-Muslims, maybe what is happening today could have been avoided.

What I'm trying to say is that what we call the past is also a lie because the injustices happening today are the price we are paying for the wrongs done then. Nothing really passes. Nothing is really in the past. Don't you see? Please see that we cannot create a more equal and just society without confronting the mistakes of the past. We do not want to be condemned to live in a swamp of lies on earth, especially in our country. As I finish, I would like to ask one question: do you want to leave a world where your children live as slaves due to the lies of the sovereigns? It has been said: "Where there is oppression, resistance is a right, and if there is a rebellion, there is oppression.

My son, do not stand by the oppressor, stand by the labor and the oppressed, so that you can live in an equal and fair world." Justice and equality are everyone's rights. Don't you think it's time to protect human dignity?

FREEDOM CONVENTION

DESPINA SYRRI

Despina Syrri is the Founder of Symbiosis-School of Political Studies in Greece, affiliated with the Council of Europe Network of Schools. She served as Education Specialist at the UNICEF Refugee and Migrant Response in Greece, Advisor to the Regional Cooperation Council Political department in Sarajevo, and Senior Expert on the Roma Integration 2020 in Belgrade. She serves as director of research and international cooperation at the Immigration Policy Institute in Greece.

Thank you for taking the time to hear and consider my thoughts. I'm the granddaughter of people that come from Synod, Kiritak, Forza, and Istanbul and today I will talk about the refugees on this side.

The refugee crisis, as we are all well aware, is far from over. The summer events in Afghanistan as well as the dramatic developments in other parts of the world that do not receive the same public attention, such as Yemen and Ethiopia, constantly endanger the lives and freedom of more people every day. These people need and are entitled to international protection as all nations have jointly agreed during the convention of Geneva, after the painful experience of World War II. This fundamental human right should not be compromised. European countries cannot and should not deny their share of responsibility for the protection of refugees.

The shift of responsibility towards other countries in exchange for financial support increases global inequalities and is morally dubious at the same time. It exposes refugees to the dangers of ill-treatment and places them in a state of limited protection. It is true that the refugee population in Greece is comparable to what happened in 2015 when over a million people crossed the Aegean sea and moved from Greece through the Balkans to Germany and Sweden. The refugee population there has been significantly reduced since 2016. Indeed thousands of people have moved to the mainland and some have left to other European countries. Nevertheless, there are women, men, and children who never made it to Greece.

Reports of serious violations of human rights taking place across European borders have been corroborated by international organizations. Many of these refugees are being pushed back to Turkey. This systematic practice endangers the lives of people including young young children that often end up abandoned in the middle of the sea. This illegal practice must end and an independent border monitoring mechanism that will investigate these events should be established.

A portion of the refugee population currently residing in Greece will remain in the country, so the Greek state has a duty to start processing a plan for their integration. Furthermore, in regard to the sharing of responsibilities, it is of utmost importance for the European Union to introduce a mandatory relocation plan similar to the one applied during 2015-17. As I mentioned before, both the number of people arriving in Greece and the number of asylum seekers living on the Greek islands have fallen sharply in the last year. Fewer than 2,500 people have reached Greece by sea so far in 2021 compared to 60,000 in the same period in 2019. The Aegean islands have gone from hosting about 2,500 people in August 2020 to 5,260 people in August 2021. Nevertheless, conditions have not improved for many vulnerable people seeking safety in Europe who still face significant and persistent barriers to access a fair asylum procedure, to dignified reception, and integration in Greece. In September the new EU-funded multi-purpose reception and identification center was set up on the Island of Summers. It is the first of five centers to be opened across the Greek islands and is considered a potential model for future facilities across Europe.

The new model, designed to keep refugees out of sight and out of mind, sees asylum seekers and refugees housed in prison-like centers in remote areas. It creates an environment that strips people of agency, decimates their mental health, and prevents them from interacting with and integrating into local communities. Authorities are also building walls around camps on the mainland to similar effects. Remaining for an extended period of time in confined facilities deprives our fellow human beings of their fundamental rights and hinders integration, which negatively impacts their daily lives and causes them severe emotional distress. Their integration into a future hosting community is a process that should begin on day one. Isolation leads to insufficient health care, social support, and even worse, leaves children deprived of proper education.

In reality, living under such circumstances mirrors a state of imprisonment. Adding to this state is the strict confinement of the asylum seekers that live in these facilities. These centers, which are exclusively funded by the European Union, should be fully reformed and their philosophy shifted to build functioning relationships between the residents and the hosting community to aid a smoother process of integration. At the same time, the fundamental human rights of asylum seekers should be protected, including access to health care and education. Above all, people should not be deprived of their freedom and dignity.

Reports from multiple sources have recorded serious allegations of >>>

FREEDOM CONVENTION

FREEDOM CONVENTION

authorities conducting push backs since March 2020. As UNHCR, the European Commission, the Council of Europe and others have stressed, these violations of international law and human rights, which have subjected individuals to mistreatment and violence, must be urgently investigated by an independent body. If the rule of law is to be upheld in Europe, the European Commission recently announced that the establishment of a mechanism to monitor human rights abuses on its borders is a precondition for the release of an additional 15.8 million euros of additional EU funding for Greece.

Refusing the entry of migrants and refugees into a country's territory and forcing them back to countries from where they escaped without lodging and or examining an asylum claim has become the regular modus operandi both at the external and internal borders of the European Union. The Greek authorities, in particular, have been repeatedly urged to investigate the accusations. Amnesty International described it as the country's de facto policy of border management. Even EU Home Affairs Commissioner Ylva Johansson has acknowledged that the findings are incredibly shocking, unacceptable, and has called for a national investigation into Frontex. Actually, a Frontex interpreter has been pushed back to Turkey. This echoes long-standing calls by the European Parliament. So a proposal for this new border mechanism investigation is part of the new pact on migration and asylum.

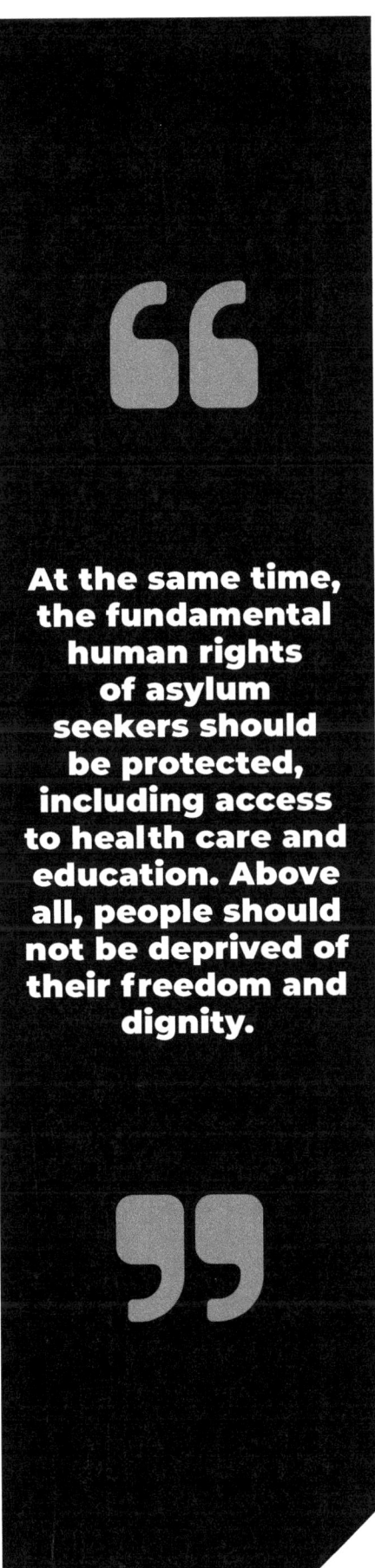

> At the same time, the fundamental human rights of asylum seekers should be protected, including access to health care and education. Above all, people should not be deprived of their freedom and dignity.

In October authorities did not distribute expected cash allowances following the government's takeover of the accommodation in cities program from UNHCR. The Guardianship Program for children and accompanied minors adopted in 2018 has not been implemented yet, while the interim one has been interrupted, leaving hundreds of children without effective representation. Access to education and health remains

patchy. So for nearly three months, now up to 60 percent of the current residents of the refugee camps in Greece on the mainland have not had access to sufficient food. Following the implementation in October 2021 of a law passed last year, the Greek government stopped providing services to those whose asylum applications have been accepted. One in four residents in these facilities are women and two in five are children. In addition, approximately 35,000 asylum seekers have gone for three months without any cash assistance and no jobs that had previously enabled them to buy food, clothing, and other essential items.

I would like to conclude by saying that by turning a blind eye to the situation, ignoring the law adopted by competent organizations and as interpreted by the courts, justice is systematically violated. Legitimizing extra-legal actions and policies are lethal to those most in need. The fundamental requirement of the rule of law is that institutions are bound by the law and judgments of the court, legally and politically. Upholding this is the most significant challenge faced by a democratic society.

www.silencedturkey.org

www.silencedturkey.org

www.ingramcontent.com/pod-product-compliance
Lightning Source LLC
Chambersburg PA
CBHW062354220526
45472CB00008B/1803